Entertaining with Gwyne

Gwyneth Dover appears regularly on television and has been featured on *TVam*, *Bazaar*, *Lifestyle Television* and the *Miriam Stoppard Show*. Her previous books are *Diet for Life*, *The New Diet for Life* and *Sweets without Sinning*. Gwyneth has also been featured on many radio programmes and has lectured on disease prevention, fitness and health alongside top heart surgeons, quite apart from giving cookery demonstrations all over Britain. In 1989 she was invited by the *Daily Telegraph* to act as diet and health expert for their pre-retirement cruises and in 1991 was fitness, diet and health lecturer for the CTC Canary Cruise.

With her husband Richard she won the 'Here's to Health' award in 1987. They live in a farmhouse in North Yorkshire which they converted themselves.

Entertaining with
GWYNETH DOVER

PAN BOOKS

LONDON, SYDNEY AND AUCKLAND

in association with

SIDGWICK & JACKSON LIMITED

First published 1992 by
PAN BOOKS LIMITED
A division of Pan Macmillan Publishers Limited
Cavaye Place London SW10 9PG
and Basingstoke
in association with Sidgwick & Jackson Limited

Associated companies throughout the world

ISBN 0 330 32546 9

1 3 5 7 9 8 6 4 2

A CIP catalogue record for this book is available from the
British Library

Typeset by Parker Typesetting Service, Leicester
Printed and bound in Great Britain by
Mackays of Chatham PLC, Chatham, Kent

The author and publishers would like to thank Josiah
Wedgwood & Sons Limited for kindly lending the
tableware used in the plate section and on the cover;
Paul Grant for his photography; and Anne Vincent
for her excellent work as a stylist.

I would like to dedicate this book, as usual, to my loving husband Richard, without whose love, support and strength of character I would never have completed it. My mum and dad also deserve much more than my thanks and sincere appreciation for the faith and confidence they have shown in me.

Sincere thanks also to my very good friends who have really helped me through a difficult time of my life. So thanks wing their way to: Mostafa and Gill; Cheryl and Herb; Josie and George; Sally and Howard; Janice and Michael; Amanda and Brett; Helen and Michael; Cathy, Ian and Alex; Neil and Fiona; Mike, Philip and Lorraine; Sue, Carol and Gill, and Mike and Madge. 'The Long Ashes Support Group' (he! he!) consisting of Elisabeth; Jan; Rachel; Vena and Don; Yvonne and Brian; Brian and Adrian.

And last, but by no means least, a very special thank you to Melvyn, who has been like a brother to me over the past year. He deserves a gold medal for endurance! Keep practising the squash, Mel (ha! ha!).

Thanks to all of you for caring enough to be there for me.

By the way – have you heard the one about . . .

ACKNOWLEDGEMENTS

I would like to take this opportunity to thank everyone concerned in the publishing of this book. My editor, Ingrid Connell, deserves special thanks for the very high standard of her work and for her good-humoured approach throughout.

My very dear friend Mostafa Hammuri has worked relentlessly on my behalf and has shown complete faith in me. Thanks for the confidence, Mostafa!

A big thank you to my very patient typist, Mary Hebden, for translating my scribble and scrawl into a legible typescript and for meeting my deadlines with a smile – despite having her tonsils out!

Oh, and I mustn't forget Norman Taylor, my friendly local Pan salesman – keep up the good work, Norm, the sandwich board is on its way!

CONTENTS

INTRODUCTION
1

CHAPTER ONE
First Things First
5

CHAPTER TWO
To the Drawing Board
8

CHAPTER THREE
Putting on the Glitz
14

CHAPTER FOUR
It'll be All Right on the Night
25

CHAPTER FIVE
Drink and be Merry – But Not Too Merry!
29

CHAPTER SIX
All Dressed Up
49

CHAPTER SEVEN
The Ingredients and the Recipes
55

CHAPTER EIGHT
A Fine Romance
64

CHAPTER NINE
Party Time
83

CHAPTER TEN
The Festive Season
128

CHAPTER ELEVEN
The Great Escape
155

INDEX
211

INTRODUCTION

To me the word 'entertaining' covers a whole range of occasions, from a humble fork supper to an engagement dinner. But whatever the occasion, the experience should be fun both for the guests and hosts alike. And basically, that is what this book is all about – taking the hassle and worry out of entertaining.

I love every aspect of entertaining: the planning, preparations, cooking, socializing and even the washing-up afterwards! Obviously, the food contributes a lot to the occasion and so it is worth putting the time and effort beforehand into deciding what to serve and how to present it to full effect. When I see my guests enjoying the food I have prepared for them it gives me such a kick I feel ten feet tall. So entertaining for me is partly a selfish act, I suppose.

Each book I have written has been very personal and this one is no exception. In it I explain how to entertain in a variety of situations from an engagement dinner to a children's party, as well as mouthwatering recipes to tempt anyone's taste-buds. I also give hints about which glasses to use for which wine, or where to put all the cutlery for the meal or how to serve the food correctly. Everything you need to know is here at your fingertips.

Needless to say, my recipes are actually good for your health as well as being delicious and elegant. Each recipe is low in fat, especially the 'bad' saturated type, low in cholesterol, low in sugar and salt but high in fibre and taste.

I realize that healthy eating considerations tend to be thrown out of the window at the very mention of entertaining. It certainly used to be the case for me years ago. But you don't suddenly have to bring out the double cream and chocolates to make impressive food: the recipes that follow prove this point.

Enjoy yourselves . . . I do!

Entertaining with
GWYNETH DOVER

First Things First

The major problem I have when I'm organizing a get-together, be it a party or a dinner, is over-enthusiasm. The whole event takes over and everything has to be spot on and done yesterday. All of a sudden I think that I'm some kind of superwoman who can achieve the impossible. And isn't it a shock to the system when reality rears its ugly head and you discover you are a mere mortal? I can remember arranging dinner parties consisting of six intricate courses, all of which had to be freshly prepared on the day. The problem was that I had a full-time job as well, which left precious little time to prepare for the party. It was just one of those minor details that flew out of my head in my enthusiasm. After coming a cropper with such lack of forethought a few times, I realized what unnecessary pressure I was placing on myself and started to think before acting – always sound advice. The moral of this cautionary tale is to think of the time element and always, always set realistic targets.

If you have no choice and have to arrange something mid-week, say a birthday party, then it is always better to compromise. You don't want to chase your own tail, dashing here and there, looking an untidy wreck and ignoring your guests because you're too busy in the kitchen.

You can easily compromise by planning the food so that at least two of the courses can be made in advance and frozen or stored in a fridge for a day or two. That will just leave minor preparation on the day itself. Alternatively, make the occasion very informal, say a late supper, that requires little preparation. Make it easy on yourself and that way you will enjoy the evening as well as your guests – and that's the whole idea, isn't it!

In my bouts of over-enthusiasm another mistake I tend to make is to plan foods and wine that are quite expensive. It doesn't look too bad when you see smoked salmon, king prawns, asparagus and an unusual little wine to accompany each course on a shopping list – it's when you come to buy these things that shivers run down your spine. And it's not necessary anyway as most people are not going to be impressed simply because of the price tag. Budget within your means and make the most of everyday, seasonal foods. Make the meal look special by clever and imaginative garnishes – presentation is crucial. Simple food tends to be enjoyed more than its fancy counterpart.

Another thing to remember is not to get carried away and invite more people than you can cope with. Keep in mind mundane things like the size of your house, how many guests your dining table can seat comfortably (leave enough space to enable elbows to move freely), the number of knives, forks and spoons you own, not to mention the crockery. All are important considerations.

Once I invited too many people to a dinner party and, unfortunately, everyone turned up. I had to extend the small dining table by fixing an old door to it with 'G' clamps. I didn't have time to take the door handles off and so, with a pretty pink sheet acting as a tablecloth, we sat around the 'table' trying to avoid the two 'G' clamps and door handle that protruded unceremoniously from it. To make matters worse the door was panelled! We had great fun that evening, as you can imagine.

Should the occasion demand large numbers then a buffet is more suitable than a sit-down affair. But once again, it does depend on the size of the rooms you have available in your home. A gathering of forty people can seem lost in some homes whilst twenty would be just too much for others.

Some gatherings, especially those centred around the family, will determine the guests you invite but often you will have a choice. It's all too easy to think that you owe two couples a meal and that a good idea would be to kill two birds with one stone and have them around together. Although it sounds reasonable you could be opening up a hornet's nest, especially if they don't know each other, so beware! At a gathering with plenty of people you don't have to think of what they have in common because there are enough present for the guests to mingle and chat with each other. The chances are that everyone will find someone to have an interesting time with. At a dinner party the situation can be quite different. Nothing is more embarrassing than silence at the table or forced chatter about the weather.

Ideally your guests should complement each other to make for a successful evening. You could be heading for disaster if you invite people with similar characters. Eight extrovert, dominant, chatty people around one table would be totally overpowering. Can you imagine all of them fighting for attention? Eight introverts would be equally bad, with no one wanting to contribute to the conversation. A mixture of the two works well – performers and audience.

Inviting people with widely different political views can make for a lively evening – if that's what you want. Such events can be quite entertaining but can easily get out of hand, especially after one or two drinks have been consumed. It's just another point to bear in mind while scratching your head wondering whom to invite. Try not to invite people who work in similar fields as this could result in an evening of 'shop talk' and nothing much else. It really is a potential mine-field so just aim for a good mix.

The next thing to consider is how to invite your guests and there are no set rules of etiquette on this. For small, adult functions a telephone call will normally suffice but do remember to keep a note of who is coming and who is not. When a larger gathering is planned I find it more convenient to send out written invitations. The pre-printed invitations with a tear-off reply section are ideal and quite inexpensive to buy. This way you will find it easier to keep a check on acceptances.

Written invitations are a necessary ingredient for a children's party – it's all part of the fun. Try letting your children make their own party invitations – with your supervision of course! A Christmas party invitation could be in the shape of a Christmas tree, a Father Christmas, a snowman or a Christmas stocking. A birthday party one could be anything from a teddy bear to a number denoting the age of the child concerned. It's all great fun.

CHAPTER TWO

To the Drawing Board

PLANNING

The secret to successful entertaining is good, well-thought-out planning. And that means making lists for everything, from who's going to be there to the number of plates needed. I must admit that I am a compulsive list-maker anyway and so this exercise is second nature to me. To some people this may seem a bit of a chore, but believe me it is a necessary one.

First of all you need a list of the guests who will be present for the occasion. At this stage, it is a good idea to remind yourself of any guest who has special dietary requirements or a dislike of certain foods. A note here about vegetarians and vegans as there seems to be quite a lot of confusion about what they actually eat. A vegetarian will eat fruit, vegetables, nuts, beans and pulses, but will not consume meat of any kind, whether it be red or white, nor will a vegetarian eat fish, shellfish or cheese containing animal rennet. (A vegetarian who eats fish is a contradiction in terms.) A vegan is a vegetarian who takes things one step further and will not consume anything that comes from an animal. That rules out eggs, dairy milk, dairy cream, butter and dairy cheese. I mention this because vegetarianism is growing and it is likely you will be confronted with such catering at some time. It is far better to know and plan for this in advance rather than let it come to light at the last moment and cause embarrassment both to the guests and host.

You should also make a list, an extensive list, of all the things that you will need to make sure you have enough of everything. It can be a nuisance to run out of plates for the pudding because you used them as side plates earlier in the meal and have to perform a quick wash-up. I have spent time doing this very task on many occasions with glasses, plates and cutlery because I did not have enough to see me through. While this is perfectly acceptable to most guests, especially if you know them well, it can prove a little embarrassing with unfamiliar people. And, of course, it means you are rushing about spending time in the kitchen instead of with your guests enjoying yourself. A way out of this dilemma is either to borrow what you need from a friend or neighbour; buy extra – although that can prove quite expensive – or simply adapt your menu accordingly in an effort to minimize the problem. For example, if you are planning on having a soup course don't make a pudding that requires a bowl. It's as easy as that.

And now for the big one – the dreaded shopping list! To make life a little easier I make lists under 'place' headings such as supermarket; fishmonger's; greengrocer's. This usually ensures that only one trip to each is required instead of trailing back and forth because you forgot something. However, let me tell you now that this is not foolproof by any means!

Do make sure that your list includes absolutely everything and in the quantities you require. Remember to take this shopping list with you to the shops at all costs. I usually spend hours making a list and then forget to take it with me. Try to avoid the temptation of overbuying by sticking rigidly to what is on your carefully compiled list. Once again, I tend to get a little carried away and buy things that I think I might need but then never do. Not only does this create a lot of waste, it is also expensive. You should never purchase things you don't really need as they are dear at any price. (I wish I could remember that one when the January sales are on!)

THE MENU

Planning a menu for any event, whatever it is, can be a daunting prospect. The menu you decide upon should take account of the occasion, the season and the number of guests who will be present.

A menu including extremely rich dishes would not be appropriate for a children's party – nor would it be appreciated. Similarly, burgers and jellies would be great for a children's party but would look totally out of place at a romantic dinner. The menu must be planned around the occasion and reflect it where possible.

Central to any menu that I may be planning will be seasonal ingredients. Not only does this ensure freshness and good quality, it is also less expensive because the ingredients are plentiful.

Clearly the number of guests will dictate, to a certain extent, your menu. A sit-down meal is not really feasible if you intend inviting thirty people. Your dining table would have to be huge! On the other side of the coin, a buffet would look silly if you only had four guests.

In an effort to impress you may fall into the trap of being too elaborate. Remember that it is better to serve fewer dishes and courses cooked and presented well than to be over-ambitious with lots of courses cooked in a mediocre fashion. Think of each course carefully but not in isolation from the rest of the menu. It's all a question of balance and harmonization. To achieve this you need to think of colours, textures, flavours and substance. Too much of the same thing becomes boring and that maxim is especially true when the taste-buds are involved.

As for colours, you have to decide whether you want contrasts or a subtle harmony. Imagine the plate as an artist's paint palette and take it from there. I would never serve potatoes with sweet-corn and parsnips as the colours together would look wishy-washy and would not tempt the taste-buds at all. A more attract-ive and appetizing colour scheme would be potatoes with broccoli and carrots. Even if the colours of the food itself look similar you can always spruce them up by the clever use of garnishes. It can make all the difference, even if it is merely a scattering of chopped fresh herbs.

Textures are another important factor to think about. If every-thing has a similar texture you will not appreciate the separate items. Serving soup is fine as long as you don't follow it with a 'saucy' main course. It's just too much of a muchness. Change the texture by serving a dryish main course; something grilled or baked would be better. A main course which has rather a liquid consistency would be better accompanied by crisp vegetables rather than puréed ones.

Serving crispy, dry foods together is just as bad – in fact, it can be worse because you can experience difficulty in swallowing the food. Serve sauces or puréed vegetables to help the food on its way a little.

Experiment with combinations of different ingredients to enhance flavours within a meal. Lemon with fish is common but what about trying orange and lime for a change? Try grating lemon zest on to broccoli florets and using herbs and spices for flavouring instead of salt. The idea is not to overpower the dish with additional flavourings but merely to embellish its natural flavour. And try not to use similar flavourings throughout your menu. A lemon and parsnip soup followed by fish in lemon sauce with a lemon soufflé to finish would be a little too much for even the most ardent lemon fan to swallow! (Excuse the pun – I couldn't resist.)

The aim of any food occasion is not to stuff your guests with so much grub that they are unable to move from the table and have to suck indigestion pills for the rest of the evening. Bear in mind how filling each course is in relation to the menu as a whole. Home-made soups are quite substantial, so try to make the main course fairly light – grilled fish rather than a chicken pie. If you are serving pastry in one of the courses don't use it again. Fresh fruit, as exotic as you like, is a useful dessert when you wish to finish with something light and refreshing.

As long as you keep these important factors at the back of your mind when planning your menu, you should be successful. Good luck!

TABLE MANNERS

Strict rules carved in stone dictated one's behaviour at dinner parties in the past and still do for formal occasions today. To begin with, when the hostess announces that everything is ready, the man should enter the dining-room with the woman on his right, and all the women should be seated before any of the men sit down. Not only that, but your seat should be a reasonable distance from the table. Someone who squeezes right up to the table or is clearly too far from the table is showing nervousness, no less.

It was strongly thought that manners counted more at the table than anywhere else and it was important not to break any of these rules of eating, yet at the same time not to look as though you were trying hard. No wonder people squeezed up to the dining table! What an ordeal – I think with those pressures I would be almost sat on the table. And it doesn't end there. Your serviette should be kept on your knee, and never tucked down your neck and never used to wipe your mouth while still rolled up.

Eating soup was, and still is, surrounded by mystique. How do you get the spoonful of soup to your lips without slurping it or dribbling it back into the bowl? Well, this is how to do it, folks. You must take up the soup by pushing the spoon horizontally away from you; never put the tip of the spoon to the mouth, use the side only. Apparently, this is to minimize your elbow movement – after all you don't want to nudge the person sitting next to you: it might make them dribble their soup. If you are tempted to tilt your soup bowl, don't (slapped knuckles for me because I always have a little tilt). But, should you insist on lifting it, you must only raise the part nearest to you. Of course, the accompanying bread should never be cut with a knife but merely broken. Oh, and you should refrain from playing with your bread, as if you would, as this shows you are uneasy.

Now for the fork. You should use a fork in a dainty manner and not as though it is a shovel. Food should be balanced, in small quantities, on the back of the prongs at the tips. And keep those elbows tucked neatly into your sides. But what about 'soggy' or 'creamy' foods, I hear you cry. After all, you can't very well balance a vindaloo and pilau rice on fork prongs, can you? Under such circumstances it is quite acceptable to use the fork with the prongs upturned, but be careful not to get carried away and use it like a navvy's shovel – easy to do with a good curry. Eating salads with a fork can prove hazardous, not to mention hilariously funny to onlookers, as you attempt to balance crunchy celery and cucumber on the prongs. Simply stab the food with the prongs instead; it's the only way to do it. Personally, I love eating salad with my fingers – it's the perfect 'finger food' and it seems to taste so much nicer. Funny, isn't it, that fish and chips always taste better when eaten in a newspaper wrapping (not that I would know, but I have it on good authority!)

Should you survive the pressure of your dinner party without throwing a wobbler then, on rising from the table, you should not fold your serviette but simply leave it 'draped' elegantly on the dining table – on the left-hand side of your place setting, of course.

I am pleased to say that most everyday events do not call for such rules of etiquette. We tend to be far less formal these days, thank goodness, and nobody will be looking for the 'mistakes' people make at the table. For me there are no strict rules of etiquette as such, just politeness and thoughtfulness. So what if you don't use your fork 'correctly'; the sun will still rise tomorrow for goodness sake! All I'm saying is have a good time, let your hair down and don't get too caught up on what's 'right' and 'wrong'.

CHAPTER THREE

Putting on the Glitz

TABLECLOTH TASTE

I love to see a well-laundered, crisp, white linen tablecloth. They look so elegant and sophisticated – a product of a bygone age. You can pick up antique linen cloths of all sizes from junk shops and jumble sales very cheaply. If you're lucky you may even find tablecloths that are heavily hand-embroidered or embellished with openwork and handworked lace. Our dining table is quite large, especially when we clamp a door to it, and needs a very large tablecloth to cover it adequately. Linen sheets and coverlets are wonderful for this and cost far less than tablecloths. Some of the coverlets can be very decorative.

An attractive effect can be created by placing a coloured cloth or sheet on the table and overlaying this with an openworked cloth. It can look very striking with bright red peeping through the cloth or subtle when pastel shades are used. You can take this colour theme a step further by using pretty ribbons, tied into large bows, pinned to the corners of the cloth, very fashionable at the moment. The Victorians used to make tablecloths with holes worked in them at the corners and for special occasion ribbons would be threaded through and made into neat bows. For a wedding white ribbon was used, for a death, black ribbon and for a christening either blue or pink, depending on the sex. A nice idea, don't you think?

For a children's party, though, laundered white linen is out – just think of the stains you'd have to try to remove! Polycotton or PVC cloths or table mats are ideal for such occasions, as they are easy to care for. Brightly coloured or patterned tableclothes are a good buy and look very attractive with colourful children's food placed on it. Think practical for such events.

Other informal occasions, such as barbecues, lend themselves to bright colours rather than pastels – but that is a purely personal view. I like to lay a bright cloth on the table and then lay a smaller, contrasting cloth diagonally over the top of it for an eye-catching effect. Perfect for outdoor events.

SERVIETTE SENSE

We owe it to the French for introducing the folded serviette to us. Before this, serviettes were simply draped over the left shoulder of diners. Folded serviettes can take many, many forms and can look quite decorative on the table. They work better when the material is lightly starched. You can fold paper serviettes but they are more awkward to work with – so be warned!

The folding process can be quite elaborate and difficult to perform. However, sometimes very simple ideas can look magic. One of my favourite ways to present a serviette is to fold it carefully into a square, tie a satin ribbon around, finish with a bow and place a pretty flower between the ribbon and serviette. It looks very elegant and sophisticated. Another simple one is to roll up a serviette, place it in a serviette ring and thread a rose bud, complete with leaf, through the ring as well.

For a romantic dinner a few years ago, I invented a novel way of presenting the serviettes. All you have to do is cut out two heart shapes (one heart per serviette) from a polystyrene ceiling tile. It should measure approximately 2 in/5 cm in length and width. Fold some narrow coloured ribbon around the outer edge of the heart shape, securing it with pins or strong glue as you go. Pin a small flower to the centre of the heart. Lay a piece of ribbon, measuring approximately 6 in/15 cm long, on the table and place the heart in the centre, securing it with a pin or with strong glue. Roll up your serviette and tie the ribbon around it, neatly showing off your heart.

Similarly, for a children's party you could make the shapes in the form of teddy bears, clowns or faces – but don't use pins, only glue. For Christmas, make Christmas trees, crackers, snowmen or a Father Christmas. They look different, colourful and are fun to make.

For more elaborate folded serviettes try one or two of these:

BISHOP'S MITRE

1   Lay the serviette flat and fold it in half, away from you. Turn the top left-hand corner down to the bottom centre and turn the bottom right-hand corner up to the centre.

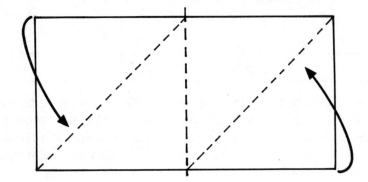

2   Turn the serviette over and with the long side in front of you, fold it in half upwards. This will form a 'W' if you release the point under the left-hand fold.

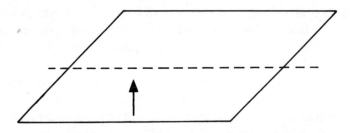

3   Fold the right-hand point in and under the diagonal fold of the left-hand section of the 'W'.

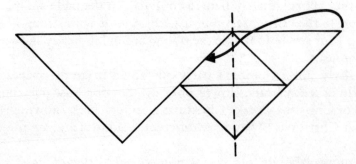

4   Finally, turn the serviette over and place the left-hand point up
    and under the diagonal fold on the other side. Stand the mitre
    up to show off its shape.

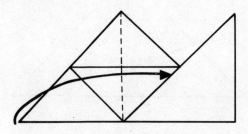

PEACOCK

1   Lay the serviette flat and fold it into four, making a square.
    Fold diagonally in half.

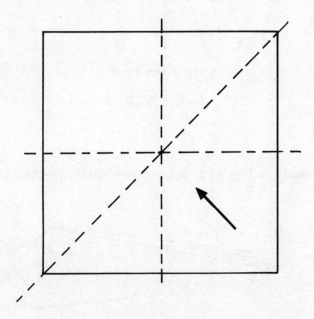

2   Fold the two outer 'triangles' into the centre.

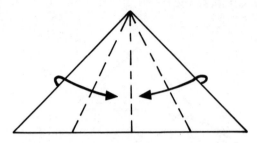

3   Fold the points underneath and fold the serviette through the centre.

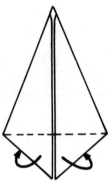

4   Carefully pull up the four leaves to form the peacock serviette.

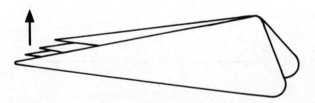

SNOWFLAKE

1   Lay the serviette flat and fold each corner until the points meet in the centre.

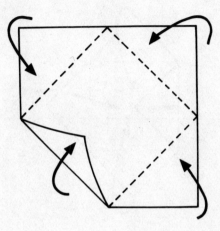

2   Repeat the process twice more without turning the serviette.

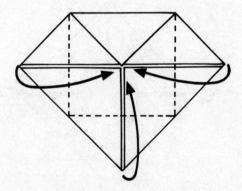

3   Turn the serviette over carefully and fold each of the corners to the centre once again, until the points meet.

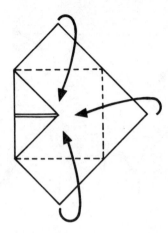

4   Hold a glass firmly in the centre of the serviette and pull each of the points, individually, away from underneath.

DUNCE'S HAT

1   Lay the serviette flat and fold the two end thirds in towards the centre third. With the plain side upwards fold the right-hand third in towards the centre.

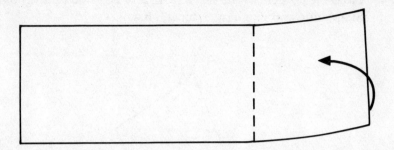

2 Hold the folded section and turn it inwards to form a cone shape.

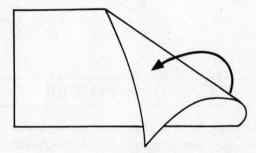

3 Fold the left-hand corner of the remaining third over to meet the point at the right.

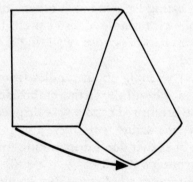

4   Hold the corners of the serviette firmly and fold up the points. Stand it up and you have a dunce's hat.

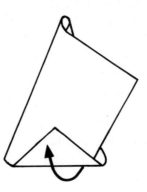

CANDLE-POWER

The most flattering light is that given by a candle for it is soft, subtle and warm. Electric lights, in contrast, tend to be severe, harsh and cold. Great for a floodlit football match but not really appropriate for a friendly get-together. So for romantic dinners candles are a must, and indeed for any evening meal where adults are seated around a dining table, I don't think you can beat them. Having said that, don't leave the table so dimly lit that nobody can see what they are eating let alone each other. Just because you are lighting your table with candles doesn't mean that the rest of the room must be in darkness; use wall lights or extra candles strategically placed.

A few words of warning about candles from my own experiences. I ruined a beautifully hand-embroidered Belgian lace tablecloth because bright red candle wax dripped repeatedly on to it. Unfortunately, the stains were there for good. Always make sure you buy the ones that don't drip; asking for non-drip candles may sound funny but it's worth it.

At a buffet a few years ago I stood candles along the full length of the table and they looked very effective. The only problem was that they were the tall ones and people kept knocking them over as they reached for the food. Luckily, the fire was put out before any real damage had been done . . . No, sorry, only joking! On a more serious note, use the short stubby little candles when people have to reach about – it's far safer.

When people are seated at a dining table it can be quite fun to watch them dodging from side to side as they try to make conversation with someone at the other side of the candlestick. Just like being at Wimbledon in fact. However, if you don't want to create this effect, it is better either to put the candles at a place on the table where they don't obstruct people's view of their fellow guests, or to choose small candles that are below eye level.

Don't worry if you don't possess any candle-holders, as you can soon improvise. For example, use an oasis (you can buy these from florists and garden centres) and surround your candles with flowers, either fresh, dried or silk (but keep the latter two away from the flame!). It makes an attractive centrepiece for the table, but do make sure that the candles are securely in place. Funnily enough, candles of varying colours look really attractive placed inside jars – any old jar you happen to have lying around the house will do. You can also try dripping a little candle wax on one or two pretty plates and standing candles of different shapes and sizes on them. The effect looks stunning. Should you happen to have a lump of wood doing nothing, why not drill holes in it to house some candles and arrange flowers around them?

FLOWERS FOR THE TABLE

A centrepiece of flowers adds that finishing touch to a well-dressed table, but try not to overdo it. Once you start a flower arrangement it can so easily get out of hand and become a monster of a thing that would look better in a garden centre than on a dining table. The idea is to enhance the table, not to be obtrusive. Clearly, the shape and size of your table will determine to a large extent what type of arrangement will best suit. A circular table looks better with a cluster of flowers whilst an oblong table will be enhanced by a long, narrow arrangement. As with the candles, keep it fairly low, and if your dining table is quite small, keep the flower arrangement small also.

One other thing to bear in mind is the kind of flowers you use for your centrepiece. Sweet peas and freesias may look pretty but their perfume is too strong and would detract from the food. Tiger lilies look exotic and colourful but the pollen drops too easily and leaves nasty stains that are hard to remove from fabric. Open roses should be avoided because their petals fall too readily. And be careful of greenfly if your flowers are hand-picked from the garden.

Dried or silk flowers can look as attractive as fresh flowers and work out cheaper in the long run as you can re-use them. You could also integrate pine cones and berries into your arrangements. For Christmas, use holly, mistletoe and small branches of pine with red bows to finish it off.

THOSE LITTLE EXTRAS

Smoking at the table is largely taboo these days but it is entirely up to you whether or not you discourage it. If you do allow smoking ensure that there are enough ashtrays on the table. Another thing to consider is how your other guests will react to the smoke and whether or not you allow it between courses or just with the coffee and liqueurs. I really do feel that smoking at the table is inconsiderate unless everyone smokes – it can spoil a meal for non-smokers. Leaving a window or a door slightly ajar will help to ventilate the room a little and minimize the smoke. It may also discourage the smokers from lighting up!

Finger bowls may be required on the table if you are serving a dish that is eaten with the fingers. Find some pretty, little, inexpensive bowls and fill them with warm water and float a sprig of mint, a lemon or lime slice or rose petals on top. You should also provide an extra napkin or something with which your guests can dry their hands.

CHAPTER FOUR

It'll be All Right on the Night

YOUR MEAL IS SERVED

The first thing you have to consider is how to set the table correctly. And I do mean correctly – there is a certain way to do it! I was brought up to work from the outside towards the inside with cutlery and that's the easiest way to remember the place setting rules. It can look very confusing, to say the least, when you are confronted with a full arsenal of knives, forks and spoons at your fingertips. And if you don't know the rules it can be quite embarrassing as you glance awkwardly at fellow guests for clues.

So let's get straight down to the basics of place settings. The easiest way to cope with cutlery is to remember that you start on the outside and work your way in! The following setting is for a full five-course meal – obviously you can adapt it to suit your menu. On the left-hand side you should have the fish fork on the outside followed by the table fork on the inside. The right-hand side consists of a starter fork on the outside, followed by a soup spoon, fish knife and on the inside a table knife. Cutlery used for the dessert is usually positioned above the place setting with the fork below the spoon. The fork handle should point to the left and the spoon handle to the right. I tend to place the butter knife diagonally across the side plate to indicate to people exactly what it is used for. The side plate goes to the left-hand side of the place setting. This assumes that all of your guests are right-handed. Simply reverse the procedure for left-handers.

On to the glassware. This is usually positioned at the top right-hand side of each place setting. But if you are anything like me, anywhere there is an inch of space available will have to do because the table is normally too crowded! Anyway, three glasses per guest are required for a full-blown sit-down meal. Two wine glasses, one for white and one for red, and a glass for water. The glasses should form a triangular cluster shape with the white wine glass placed just above the table knife, the red wine glass to the right and just behind while the water glass takes a back position just to the left of the red wine glass.

Serving the food to your guests is where the fun really starts. Tradition dictates that you serve food from the left-hand side and it's a good idea, if you are passing dishes from which guests help themselves, to place the handles of the serving spoons towards the guest. This avoids having sleeves dangling in the food. If, on the other hand, you are serving the meal already presented on the plate be very careful not to overfill it as it could easily slide off on to a lap. This is especially important where sauces and soups are concerned as they are easy to spill at any time. Well, they are for me anyway! A cold first course can be placed on the table just prior to the guests sitting down but hot food should be brought in once the guests are settled to avoid it cooling down. Once again, I am assuming your guests are right-handed and not southpaws – just do the opposite for the latter.

Sometimes it makes a change for your guests to help themselves to the food, which can be placed on the table in serving dishes. The rule here is that the serving dishes should be passed around the table in an anti-clockwise direction. That doesn't mean to say that things can't get a little chaotic! I don't know whether it's the effect I have on people or what, but guests at my dinners don't wait around for convention, they just dig in willy-nilly. But that's all right with me – rules are meant to be bent a little! Just feel at ease and enjoy yourselves.

What I find more of a problem than serving the food is keeping it hot until it is required. I maintain, very strongly, that hot food should be just that – hot – and never lukewarm. There is nothing less appetizing in my opinion. Many alternatives are open to the discerning host or hostess. Probably the most popular in recent years is the hostess trolley which is extremely useful. An added advantage is that you can also keep your plates reasonably hot at the same time. Foods such as jacket potatoes, most vegetables and garlic breads can be wrapped in foil and kept in a hot oven until required. The easiest way to keep sauces and soups hot is to use a double saucepan, or *bain-marie* as it is sometimes called. These are invaluable in the kitchen and the sauces will not turn lumpy or dry up. The bottom pan holds simmering water while the top, lidded pan holds the sauce or soup. Microwave cookers are perfect for keeping foods hot but I find the real beauty of them is their quickness. You can literally cook vegetables within minutes and thereby eliminate the need for keeping food hot. This quick cooking also means that the vitamins and minerals are retained. Those little electric hotplates, and the ones which hold small candles, which Indian and Chinese restaurants use are quite effective. These have the added advantage of being on the dining table, enabling your guests to help themselves to seconds or thirds . . .

THE AFTERMATH

Clearing the table between courses should never be rushed. It is better to sit and chat for a while and give your stomach time to recover and ready itself for the next onslaught of goodies. 'Resting' time is important and it also makes for a more relaxed atmosphere.

Once the meal is finished it is usual for some of the guests to offer their services in the kitchen and it is entirely up to you whether or not you take them up on it. From my own experiences, I prefer just to pile the dishes up in the kitchen and leave them until the guests have gone home. I find that helpers, no matter how good their intentions may be, usually turn out to be more of a hindrance. After all, you cannot expect your guests to know where things are in your kitchen and by the time you've explained you could have done it yourself anyway. And there is still the social obligation when you are in the kitchen working and so making conversation comes into play. Personally, I just like to get on with it on my own as quickly as possible. One good thing about not accepting help is that you don't feel too obliged to help at their homes. What's sauce for the goose is sauce for the gander!

WHO SITS WHERE

The hub of a successful gathering is the conversations that occur spontaneously and you can help this along by a clever seating plan. With fairly informal events I always separate partners and close friends otherwise you could easily fall into the trap of 'paired only' conversations that leave the rest of the guests isolated.

What I attempt to do is sit chatty, outgoing people next to shy introverts in the hope that the former can keep things going. It usually does work. However, if you notice long silent pauses developing, dive in and help things along a little. The more formal event should have the host at one end of the dining table and the hostess at the opposite end. The most important female present should be seated to the right of the host and the most important male seated to the right of the hostess. It is wise for the person doing most of the fetching and carrying to be seated nearest to the kitchen, for obvious reasons. The remaining partner is left at the table keeping up the conversations and enjoyment. But always remember that there is a wide gulf between the brilliant conversationalist and the everlasting talker! It's like walking a tightrope, so beware.

CHAPTER FIVE

Drink and be Merry – But Not Too Merry!

APERITIFS

Buying aperitifs can be quite expensive if you try to cater for everyone's tastes. Just think of all the bottles of spirits you would require, not to mention the mixer drinks. It's just impractical even to think of it for normal, everyday entertaining, and it's not expected.

My approach is very simple. I have two types of sherry, a medium and a dry, a cocktail already prepared and a variety of soft drinks such as mineral water and orange juice. There is always something for everyone, I find. Do ensure that there is plenty of ice and slices of citrus fruits for the drinks. Try not to get carried away by refilling your guests' glasses without them knowing – they will probably be driving home afterwards!

WINE

Thank goodness that much of the snobbery once associated with wine has largely disappeared. Wines from all over the world are now readily available from supermarkets and corner shops, not only from exclusive wine merchants. And the price of wine these days reflects its wide availability. A decent bottle of wine is well within the reach of most people.

Wine is a very personal thing and although certain suggestions can be made about which wines should be drunk with what foods, there are no hard and fast rules. Not too many years ago the general rule was white wine with fish and white meat, red wine with red meat and the line was not crossed. Things have changed a lot and now anything goes. If you enjoy a red wine with trout, that's fine – after all they are your taste-buds!

STORING WINE

Traditionally, wines have been stored in cellars and for good reason. Cellars provide the perfect environment – they are fairly cool with a constant temperature, no bright lights and draught-free. I know that most of us don't have cellars and so a compromise is required. Any spare space can be utilized: the cupboard under the stairs, the spare bedroom or a wine rack in the kitchen are all possibilities. Ideally, the temperature should be kept constant at 13°C/55°F but a few degrees either side won't do much harm.

It is most important that all wine should be laid on its side to keep the cork moist thus stopping shrinkage, and to allow any sediment to settle while it is resting.

SERVING WINE

Red wines are traditionally served at room temperature. But what is room temperature? A centrally heated house today is much warmer than a house of a hundred years ago when this guideline was made. Room temperature in those days meant only a couple of degrees warmer than the cellar itself. As a consequence of this misleading term, red wine is often served too warm, making it lifeless and tasting a little heavier than it should. I actually find that placing a bottle of red wine in the refrigerator for about thirty minutes is beneficial. Usually red wines in our houses are served at a temperature between 12°C/54°F and 15°C/59°F. Younger, lighter red wines, such as Beaujolais, are better served at the cooler end of the scale, the older, heavier types, like Bordeaux or Burgundy, at the warmer end.

You must have heard the expression 'red wines need to breathe before drinking'. In our house, at times, the red wine is lucky if it has a quick gasp! But, generally speaking, red wines should be opened at least an hour before serving.

A rosé wine (my particular favourite is Anjou Rosé) is far nicer served chilled and so I pop the bottle in the refrigerator for a couple of hours before serving it.

White wines are best served cold – but beware for if you chill the wine too much you kill the flavour completely. Some of the white wines that I have tasted in pubs would have benefited from being over-chilled! The sweeter dessert wines and sparkling wines need about three hours in the refrigerator to get them to a serving temperature of between 4°C/39°F and 6°C/43°F. Champagne and the majority of dry and medium-dry white wines require only a couple of hours, at the most, in the refrigerator. A temperature ranging from 7°C/46°F to 10°C/50°F is ideal for such wines, and will not kill the taste. Burgundy and other classic rich, dry whites are enhanced by serving them a little warmer still, at about 12°C/54°F. Not too long ago I over-chilled a good Burgundy and I had the brainwave of popping it into the microwave for a few minutes to warm it up. Sounds a reasonable idea, doesn't it? Unfortunately, I forgot to reduce the setting from high and ended up almost boiling it! In future, I will be more cautious and stand the wine in a bucket of tepid water.

There are a set of guidelines concerning the order in which you should serve wine. In this particular case it isn't snobbery but good sense because following the rules makes it better for your taste-buds – you will actually appreciate each wine. Basically, you start off with the lighter wines first and work up to the heavier ones. Dry wines are served before sweet wines, white before red, light before heavy, young before old and always keep the finer wines until last.

DECANTING AND POURING WINE

To be perfectly honest, I do not feel that decanting wine is necessary in the majority of cases. Old ports and old wines may require decanting to remove any sediment that has formed over the years. The only other time would be if you crumbled the cork into the wine by mistake when opening it.

The process of decanting is fairly straightforward. All you do is open the bottle of wine carefully, and slowly pour the wine through a coffee filter into a decanter. Handle the wine with care as the decanting process can disturb and spoil it.

After opening the bottle of wine, be sure to wipe the neck of the bottle with a clean cloth to remove any traces of dust or cork or lead from the foil that may be present. And so that drips don't dribble down the bottle and on to the tablecloth, place a spare napkin around the bottle as you pour. You can actually buy a 'barman' bottle cover complete with dicky bow-tie and striped apron which looks quite effective. Wine should be served from the guests' right-hand side and the glass should not be over-filled. In fact, a third to half full is ideal as this allows the aroma to develop and that's an important part of any wine.

ORGANIC WINES

Organic wines form only a small part of the total market for wine but their popularity is growing all the time. Scares about 'anti-freeze' in Austrian, German and Italian wines during the mid 1980s gave added impetus to the organic wine producers of the world. You can even find organic wines on supermarket shelves nowadays and at reasonable prices. The organic wines I have tasted have been of excellent quality and certainly worth trying.

The aim of organic wine-producing is to avoid the use of chemicals, in any form, on the soil, vines and in the winery. Natural methods and ingredients are used to encourage the 'right' type of insects on to the vines to protect them from disease and rot.

Unfortunately, standards throughout the wine-growing world are not uniform and by no means trustworthy. There is no yard-stick available to help you know which wines are more organic than others. Some retailers actually specify which of the wines they sell conform to the organic code, and most wine shops will offer advice when asked.

LOW-ALCOHOL WINE

Of course, you do have another option and that is to serve low-alcohol or de-alcoholized wines. You will find quite a good selection available at supermarkets and wine merchants, although, obviously, the choice is more limited than for 'normal' wines. The majority of these wines do taste quite good, and are extremely useful for those people not wishing to consume too much alcohol but who still enjoy the taste of wine. Major wine-producing countries, such as France, Germany, America and Italy, offer a full range of low-alcohol wine – dry, medium and sweet whites, rosés and reds. The alcohol level by volume varies from between 0.05 per cent, which is virtually alcohol-free, to around 5 per cent. It is useful to keep one or two bottles at the ready – just in case.

COCKTAILS

The prohibition years of the 1920s and early 1930s in America saw the invention of the cocktail, and it has been popular ever since. Bootleg liquor, although potent, was not too pleasant to drink. Cocktails allowed other flavours to dominate, making the bootleg liquor much more acceptable. Since then hundreds of cocktails have been developed and named after the oddest things.

A 'Harvey Wallbanger' was named after a chap called Harvey who drank this particular cocktail and walked into a wall on his way out of the bar. Can you believe it! The cocktail 'Kokuma' owes its existence to two very dear friends of mine, Josie and George, who named their house Kokuma and invented a cocktail for the housewarming. What a nice, romantic idea.

Generally speaking the 'Singapore Sling' is the cocktail I remember fondly – or don't remember if I'm perfectly honest. Richard and I sipped one or two of these at the Raffles Hotel where they were invented, in Singapore, a few years ago. After the first two my memory faded – I did enjoy them though!

Cocktails are fun drinks that are, at the same time, elegant and sophisticated. Unlike the cocktails served to Del Boy in *Only Fools and Horses*, which look to be part of a David Bellamy nature programme, they are best served simply with an orange twist or olive.

One of the essentials for good cocktails is plenty of ice, crushed, cracked and cubed. Crushed ice is easily made by placing some ice cubes into a polythene bag and smashing it repeatedly with a rolling pin. It's great therapy for a bad mood! Cracked ice, or broken ice, can be made in a similar way but only bashed a couple of times.

Chilled glasses are another necessity for the perfect cocktail. Ideally cocktail glasses should be placed in the refrigerator, or freezer, for about five minutes prior to use. And, to be really into the cocktail mentality, you should possess a cocktail shaker for that all-important 'shake'. Actually, a jam jar works just as well but is a little less impressive. Have plenty of lemon, orange and lime slices on hand as well as olives and mint sprigs for that final touch. And don't forget the colourful bendy straws, umbrellas, sparklers and streamers – oops, sorry, I'm getting carried away here!

Cocktails don't have to be expensive; in fact they can work out to be quite reasonable. For a large gathering make a good quantity of two different cocktails – one alcoholic and the other alcohol-free. That way you don't have to stock up on a lot of spirits. All the recipes here make one glass.

ALCOHOLIC COCKTAILS

PINK GIN

4 drops Angostura bitters
ice cubes
1 measure dry gin
iced water

Put the Angostura bitters into a cocktail glass and swirl it around until the sides are well coated. Add a couple of ice cubes followed by the gin and iced water to taste.

BUCKS FIZZ

3 fl oz/75 ml freshly squeezed orange juice, chilled
champagne or sparkling white wine, chilled

Pour the orange juice into a champagne glass and top up with the champagne or sparkling wine.

KIR

1 measure crème de cassis
dry white wine, chilled

Place the crème de cassis in a cocktail glass and top up with wine.

KIR ROYALE

1 measure crème de cassis
champagne, chilled

Pour the crème de cassis into a fluted glass and top up with champagne.

SINGAPORE SLING

2 fl oz/50 ml gin
½ lemon, juice of
1 fl oz/25 ml cherry brandy
ice cubes, cracked
sparkling mineral water or soda water, chilled
1 lemon slice
1 mint sprig

Give the gin, lemon juice and cherry brandy a good shake with the ice cubes. Pour into a tall tumbler and top up with the mineral water. Garnish with the lemon slice and mint sprig.

WHITE LADY

ice cubes
1 fl oz/25 ml gin
1 fl oz/25 ml Cointreau or Triple Sec
1 fl oz/25 ml fresh lemon juice
1 orange slice

Put the ice into a cocktail shaker and add the gin, Cointreau and lemon juice. Shake well and strain into a cocktail glass. Garnish with the orange slice. (Normally an egg white is added to give the cocktail more body. I have omitted it because of the salmonella danger of using raw egg.)

HARVEY WALLBANGER

crushed ice
2 fl oz/50 ml vodka
4 fl oz/125 ml fresh orange juice
1 measure Galliano liqueur

Two-thirds fill a tall tumbler with crushed ice and pour on the vodka, orange juice and Galliano. Stir well and serve with a drinking straw.

Bloody Mary

ice cubes
2 fl oz/50 ml vodka
4 fl oz/125 ml tomato juice
1 tbsp fresh lemon juice
1 tsp Worcestershire sauce
2 dashes Tabasco
pinch of celery salt
black pepper

Place the ice cubes, with the vodka, tomato juice, lemon juice, Worcestershire sauce, Tabasco and celery salt in a jug and stir well. Add black pepper to taste. Stir and strain into a tall tumbler.

Brandy Alexander

cracked ice
1 fl oz/25 ml brandy
1 fl oz/25 ml crème de cacao
1 fl oz/25 ml natural yogurt
pinch of freshly grated nutmeg

Shake together the cracked ice, brandy, crème de cacao and yogurt. Strain and pour into a cocktail glass. Grate a little nutmeg on the top.

Manhattan

cracked ice
2 fl oz/50 ml whisky
1 measure dry vermouth
2 drops Angostura bitters

Put the cracked ice into a cocktail glass. Mix together the whisky, vermouth and Angostura bitters and pour over the ice. Stir once. For a sweeter cocktail you could use sweet vermouth instead of the dry.

BRONX

cracked ice
3 fl oz/75 ml gin
1 fl oz/25 ml dry vermouth
1 fl oz/25 ml sweet vermouth
1 fl oz/25 ml fresh orange juice

Put all the ingredients into a cocktail shaker and shake until well mixed and chilled.

JOHN COLLINS

cracked ice
1 measure gin
1 tbsp lemon juice
1 tsp caster sugar
soda water to top up

Two-thirds fill a tall glass with the ice and pour in the remaining ingredients. Stir once.

PEACHED

crushed ice
3 fl oz/75 ml peach juice
3 fl oz/75 ml champagne, or sparkling wine

Place the ingredients into a cocktail shaker and shake until well mixed and chilled.

CHAMPAGNE COCKTAIL

2 drops of Angostura bitters
½ measure brandy
ice cubes
champagne, or sparkling wine, chilled
orange slice

Place the Angostura bitters and brandy in a fluted champagne glass with two ice cubes. Top up with chilled champagne and garnish with the orange slice.

SCREWDRIVER

ice cubes
1 measure vodka
3 measures fresh orange juice

Two-thirds fill a tall glass with ice cubes and shake the vodka and
orange juice together before pouring it over the ice cubes.

DRY MARTINI

cracked ice
2 fl oz/50 ml dry gin
1 measure dry vermouth
1 olive
1 strip of lemon rind

Place some cracked ice into a cocktail glass and pour the gin and
vermouth over. Garnish with the olive and lemon rind.

KOKUMA

cracked ice
1 measure Amaretto
2 fl oz/50 ml fresh orange juice
champagne or sparkling white wine, chilled

Place the cracked ice, Amaretto and orange juice in a cocktail
shaker and shake well until chilled. Strain into a champagne glass
and top up with the chilled champagne.

STREGA CROSSWARD

cracked ice
1 measure white rum
1 measure gin
1 measure Strega
2 measures grapefruit juice
1 orange slice
1 sprig of fresh mint

Half fill a tall glass with the cracked ice. Mix together the rum,
gin, Strega and grapefruit juice before pouring over the ice. Decorate with the orange slice and mint.

SEAWITCH

ice cubes
2 measures Strega
1 measure blue curaçao
3 measures dry sparkling wine, chilled

Place all the ingredients in a cocktail shaker and shake until chilled.
Pour into a tall glass.

NON-ALCOHOLIC COCKTAILS

PUSSYFOOT

crushed ice
1 measure lemon juice
1 measure orange juice
1 measure lime juice
1 tsp grenadine
1 cocktail cherry

Place the ice, juices and grenadine into a cocktail shaker and shake
well. Pour into a tall glass and add the cherry for garnish.

CINDERELLA

cracked ice
2 measures lemon juice
2 measures pineapple juice
2 measures orange juice

Shake together and pour into a tall glass.

BUBBLES

ice cubes
3 measures peach juice
sparkling mineral water

Half fill a tall glass with ice cubes and pour on the peach juice. Top
up with the mineral water and stir.

Orange Fizz

crushed ice
4 fl oz/125 ml orange juice, freshly squeezed
soda water, chilled

Two-thirds fill a tall glass with the crushed ice and pour over the orange juice. Top up with the soda water and stir.

Ginger Refresher

cracked ice
3 measures orange juice, freshly squeezed
ginger ale, chilled

Two-thirds fill a tall glass with the ice and pour on the orange juice. Top up with the ginger ale and stir once.

Applejack

crushed ice
4 measures apple juice
½ tsp ground cinnamon
soda water or sparkling mineral water, chilled

Place the ice, apple juice and cinnamon in a cocktail shaker and shake until chilled. Pour into a tall glass and top up with the soda water.

GLASSES

Tradition dictates that certain drinks are served in a particular shape of glass. Sometimes there is a reason behind the tradition and sometimes not and, once again, the tradition is not carved in stone. If you don't happen to possess the 'right' shape of glass don't panic, the sky won't fall in!

Sherry glass: a small tulip-shaped glass, or schooner, on a stubby stem, a size smaller than a wine glass.

Cocktail glass: a tall slender stem with a cone-shaped bowl is the classic, very angular, shape. The long stem has a use: it means that your hand can't melt the ice in the drink.

Tall tumbler: perfect for certain cocktails and mixer drinks that require plenty of ice.

Small chubby tumbler: ideal for short drinks like whisky and for fruit juices.

Champagne flute: the only shape of glass in which to serve champagne or sparkling wine, as the bubbles are retained by the narrowness.

White wine glass: usually the glass has a tall and slender stem and the bowl is a tulip shape. Once again the idea of the tall stem is to keep the warmth of the hand from the chilled wine.

Red wine glass: a medium-length stemmed glass with a wide, deep bowl is the ideal shape for red wines served at room temperature. The warmth of your hand around the glass keeps the wine warm and the wide bowl allows the aroma to be appreciated.

Liqueur glass: tiny glasses, usually a tulip shape.

Port glass: traditionally port is served in a glass similar to a sherry type but with a shorter stem.

Brandy: a large balloon-shaped glass with a short stem – perfect for nestling in the palms of your hands to give it warmth and to allow the aroma to develop.

AFTER DINNER DRINKS

Only on the most formal of occasions, or in aristocratic circles, will you find that 'passing the port' remains an important part of the dining process. We now have plenty of choices in the way of after dinner drinks besides the traditional port.

Brandy remains extremely popular and ever fashionable. So too does a good malt whisky, Richard's favourite tipple. Soda, dry ginger and ice should be on offer as well. Madeira is a very pleasing drink after a meal as is marsala – both tend to be popular with females. Two liqueurs which are 'in vogue' at the moment are Strega, an Italian drink made from over seventy rare herbs, which is considered to be an excellent digestive, and sambuca, again from Italy: made from the elder shrub, it is traditionally briefly flamed before drinking.

The very sweet, highly coloured and sticky liqueurs are, thankfully, not the 'in thing' these days. So it is not really necessary to keep the cherry brandy and crème de menthe in the store cupboard.

COFFEE

I really enjoy a good cup of coffee and I do stress 'good'. All too often coffee comes straight out of a jar and bears little resemblance to the freshly ground variety. Don't get me wrong, instant coffee does have a role to play in our busy day-to-day lives, but for offering to others, and when we have the time, ground coffee is a must.

There are so many varieties and types of coffee available that it can be quite confusing. I have definite favourites but I do go through fads of drinking one variety for weeks and then suddenly change to another. As with anything else, coffee drinking is a very personal affair and what suits one person will not suit another.

Probably my all-time favourite is a coffee I first tasted at Betty's Tea Rooms in Ilkley – Sumatra Mandheling: a beautifully rich, mellow coffee with a smoothness reminiscent of chocolate.

The finest coffee in the world is reputed to be Jamaica Blue Mountain Peaberry – it is probably the most expensive too! It has smooth, mellow body and is worth at least one try. A very dear friend of mine, Mostafa Hammuri, will only drink this particular coffee and he actually grinds a few cardamom seeds in with the coffee beans. The aroma is out of this world and the taste is exquisite. I know that it sounds an unlikely combination but it really does work well.

Hawaiian Kana Kai is the coffee to buy if you like a fruity flavour balanced with a rich, full body. A well-rounded, full-bodied coffee which is as smooth as silk is Celebes Kalossi – a medium roast from the Island of Celebes, near Borneo.

The range of special, rare coffees that is now available is vast and it is fun to try different coffees from all over the world. But don't get carried away and buy lots and lots all at once – your bank balance will take a long time to recover. For everyday fresh coffee drinking, I tend to go for a medium roast decaffeinated bean with a full flavour. Do make sure that the decaffeinated coffee you buy has used the water, and not the chemical, process for removing the caffeine. Although the latter method is just as efficient at removing the caffeine, chemicals are left behind which are worse for our health than the caffeine! This also applies to instant coffees, so read the labels carefully.

If you own a coffee grinder of some sort, it is always better to buy coffee beans and grind them yourself in small quantities as you require. This way the full flavour of the coffee is retained. Some people think that if you don't possess a percolator, filter machine or a cafetière you can't make coffee. Well, you can and all you need is a jug, saucer and strainer. This is the old-fashioned method of making coffee. Warm the jug thoroughly, place some coffee grounds in the bottom and simply fill up with boiling water, put the saucer on the top and leave to infuse for about five minutes. Strain into coffee cups and serve. Couldn't be easier!

Warmed skimmed milk is always served with coffee in our home. Cold milk chills the coffee too much. If you want to drink your coffee with cream then why not try a half-fat type – there is nothing wrong with a compromise! When it comes to sugars, people seem to prefer the flavour of the brown varieties; offering sugar crystals is the done thing whilst sugar lumps are definitely a no-no these days.

TEA

Tea is not one of my favourite drinks I'm afraid, and so I have enlisted the help of my husband Richard – a fervent tea drinker. According to Richard, nothing quenches the thirst, or is more refreshing, than a cup of tea. For everyday drinking, one of the blended leaf teas is quite acceptable but for entertaining purposes, try something a little different.

A strong-flavoured tea that Richard likes is Tippy Assam, whereas I much prefer the more subtle, scented Earl Grey tea. Darjeeling is a pleasant compromise between the two. Leaf tea can also be bought blended with flowers and fruit zest – very exotic. I must say that the aroma is always more pungent than the taste, but they are quite refreshing. China Rose Petal, Japanese Cherry

Blossom and Passion Flower are amongst the most popular. Orange Pekoe is a lovely fruity tea and you can buy lemon, grapefruit and lime too. Peppermint Tisane I really do enjoy – the taste is strong and it really cleanses the palate. A lovely side effect of this particular tea is that it fills the whole room with the most wonderful aroma. Quite often these subtle, mellow teas make a very welcome change from the more 'ordinary' blended teas.

Teas which I do drink quite often are the herbal fruit ones. Unlike the fruity blended teas, they do not contain any leaf tea. In fact they are a careful blend of fruit and flowers that have a beautifully fragrant quality. They are like pure nectar! And they are naturally caffeine-free. You can purchase many varieties including Wild Raspberry, Wild Strawberry, Wild Blackcurrant and Lemon Grove. Good health shops carry a large stock of these increasingly popular teas.

As with coffee, there is a certain 'right' way to make good tea. You must warm the teapot well before adding the required amount of tea. Make sure that the water you 'mash' the tea with is boiling and then give it a stir around. Leave the tea to brew for about five minutes before pouring. Serve both skimmed milk and lemon slices to give people a choice with their tea.

WINE AND FOOD

FOOD	WINE CHARACTERISTICS	WINE EXAMPLES	CRISP, DRY WHITE	MEDIUM, DRY WHITE	SWEET WHITE	CHAMPAGNE	LIGHT RED	MEDIUM RED	CLARET	ROSÉ
Hors d'oeuvres – hot	Light wines on the dry side	Pouilly Blanc Fumé; Pinot Blanco; Gordolino	✓	✓			✓			✓
Hors d'oeuvres – cold	Bone-dry, fresh light wines	Sauvignon; Beaujolais; Rioja Rosé	✓			✓	✓			✓
Soup	Dry, light wines with a simple flavour	Pinot Blanc d'Alsace; Chianti; Hungarian or USA Pinot Noir	✓				✓			✓
Fish – hot	Light wines with a low level of acidity	Soave; Frascati; Portuguese Rosé	✓	✓						✓
Fish – cold	Dry, lighter-bodied wines	Pouilly Blanc Fumé	✓			✓				✓

FOOD	WINE CHARACTERISTICS	WINE EXAMPLES	CRISP, DRY WHITE	MEDIUM, DRY WHITE	SWEET WHITE	CHAMPAGNE	LIGHT RED	MEDIUM RED	CLARET	ROSÉ
Shellfish	Bone-dry, rich wines	Chardonnay; Muscadet; Côtes du Rhône Rosé	✓			✓				✓
Chicken and turkey	Fruity, dryish wines – light	Riesling; Sauvignon; Lambrusco Rosso	✓	✓			✓			
Duck and goose	Fruity reds	Pinot Noir; Beaujolais; Cabernet Sauvignon						✓	✓	
Game	Spicy, full-bodied reds	Zinfandel; Australian Shiraz; St Emilion						✓	✓	
Venison	Spicy reds	Nebbiolo d'Alba; Crozes Hermitage						✓	✓	

Food	Wine description	Wine examples	1	2	3	4	5	6	7	8
Rabbit	Simple-flavoured country wines	Chianti; Anjou Rosé					✓			✓
Beef	Full-bodied, rich reds with lots of character and crisp dry whites	Barolo; Côte Rôtie; Chablis; Chardonnay	✓					✓	✓	
Veal	Light wines with simple flavours	Soave; Frascati; Beaujolais	✓				✓			✓
Lamb and pork	Rich, red wines and full-flavoured dry whites	Côtes du Rhône; Rioja; Pinot Blanc	✓				✓	✓		
Desserts	Rich, fruity wines for fruity desserts and very sweet for creamy desserts	Muscats; Sweet Riesling; Sauternes; Eiswein			✓	✓				
Cheese	Gentle, fruity reds and bone-dry whites with full flavour	Burgundy; Chablis; Chardonnay; Entre-deux-Mers	✓					✓	✓	
Chinese food	A tasty, full-flavoured white wine on the dry side	Chablis; Chardonnay	✓	✓						

FOOD	WINE CHARACTERISTICS	WINE EXAMPLES	CRISP, DRY WHITE	MEDIUM, DRY WHITE	SWEET WHITE	CHAMPAGNE	LIGHT RED	MEDIUM RED	CLARET	ROSÉ
Indian food	Inexpensive wines which are fruity or spicy. Champagne is great!	Rieslings; Bardolino; Orvieto Secco; Asti Spumanti	✓			✓	✓			
Thai food	A rich, full-bodied wine	Sauvignon Blanc; Mosel Kabinett; Mateus Rosé	✓	✓						✓
Japanese food	Rich, dry whites with lots of taste	White Burgundy; Hermitage; Côtes du Rhône	✓	✓		✓				✓
Vegetarian food	Bone-dry wines with a fruity flavour	Muscadet; Cabernet Sauvignon; Chiaretto di Bardolino	✓			✓	✓			✓

CHAPTER SIX

All Dressed Up

I am always impressed by prettily garnished food. It shows that someone cares about how the food looks and that, to me anyway, is so important. Usually the first thing to arouse us in food is its appearance, then its aroma and finally its taste. First impressions are always the most striking.

Contrary to popular belief garnishes don't have to be very complicated and time-consuming to prepare. Quite often the simplest of garnishes can be the most effective. A feathery sprig of dill, a drop of yogurt swirled into a star shape or the zest of lime can all look super and add that special finishing touch that makes all the difference. Fruit, vegetables, herbs, pastry, bread, nuts – even flowers and leaves – can all be used as garnish. The three things to keep in mind are shape, colour and texture.

VEGETABLES

MUSHROOM CATHERINE WHEELS

Button mushrooms are ideal for this garnish but do ensure that they are fresh, firm and without blemish. Carefully wipe each mushroom with a damp cloth and, using a very sharp knife, cut curved ridges into the mushroom cap working from the centre to the outer edge. Continue around the mushroom removing the cut flesh as you go. They should look like petals or Catherine wheels. Cut off the stems level with the caps. Gently sauté the mushroom caps in a little low-fat cooking spread and a few drops of lemon juice. Serve either hot or cold.

LOTUS BLOSSOM

Lotus root is a popular Asian vegetable with a crisp texture and a creamy colour. But the one thing that makes it perfect for a garnish is its natural attractive pattern – it has holes running through it just like Gruyère cheese. It's wonderful! You can buy it in cans from Asian food shops and in some supermarkets. Drain the lotus root well and cut into thin slices. By cutting out pieces of the lotus root between the holes on the outer edge you will enhance the effect. I like the natural creamy colour of the lotus root but you could, if you wished, pop the slices into water that has a few drops of food colouring added.

TOMATO FLOWERS

You can use tiny cherry tomatoes for this garnish or, if you prefer a larger 'flower', a normal-sized tomato could be used. The tomatoes must be very firm and a sharp knife must be used. Hold the tomato stem side down and carefully make cuts in the skin only across the centre of the tomato and three-quarters of the way down the sides. Repeat this process, working your way around the tomato giving you eight 'segments' in all. Very carefully peel the skin 'petals' away from the tomato flesh with the knife, almost to the base. The 'petals' will spread outwards forming a flower shape. Place a currant or herb sprig in the centre of the tomato flower.

TOMATO CUPS

Again you can use cherry or normal-size tomatoes for this garnish. The same process of cutting is involved as above, except this time the cuts go right through the tomato almost to the base – the base in effect becomes the fringe. Just give a little gentle pressure on the 'wedges' to spread them out giving a cup effect.

COURGETTE FANS

Wipe the courgette and cut it in half lengthways. Slice off the end with a diagonal cut and, following this line, make seven paper-thin slices, being careful not to cut all the way through until the seventh slice so that one side of the courgette acts as a hinge. Bend every second slice back to the hinged side, leaving alternate slices straight. If the slices break you have made the slices too thick – they must be tissue paper thin.

Courgette Cogs

Wipe the courgette and cut each end off. Using a fork score all round along the length of the courgette and cut into slices with a sharp knife.

Radish Roses

Try to buy even-sized radishes with a good colour and firm texture. Remove the stem and excess stalk. Using a very sharp knife cut paper-thin slices from the top, in a petal shape, to just over halfway down the radish, being careful to keep the slices attached to the radish at the base of the cut. Repeat this process, working around the radish. Plunge in iced water and leave for 30 minutes or until the 'flowers' open up.

Radish Fans

Trim off the stalk and stem. With a sharp knife make very thin cuts across the radish, taking great care not to cut all the way through. You need to leave a slight hinge at the base of the radish. Drop the radishes into iced water and leave for a couple of hours to open up.

Cucumber Curls

Using a potato peeler cut paper-thin strips of cucumber peel about 6 in/15 cm long. Plunge into iced water for an hour to curl.

Cucumber Fans

Cut the cucumber in half lengthways and place it cut side down on a work surface. Using a sharp knife make paper-thin slices across the cucumber, not all the way through, until you get to the tenth slice, and then slice all the way across. The tenth slice will separate the fan from the cucumber. Continue until you have as many fans as you require. Fan out the cucumber with your fingers for the garnish.

Spring Onion Whisks

Cut off the top green end from the spring onions, leaving a bulb end of about 4 in/10 cm long. Using a sharp knife cut through the length of the spring onion at regular intervals but leaving the white bulb intact. Plunge into iced water for an hour to open up.

Carrot Roses

Peel the carrots thinly. Using a potato peeler cut long spirals from the carrot. Twist each spiral around your finger to form a 'rose' shape. Secure each one with a cocktail stick. Plunge into iced water for 30 minutes or so.

Celery Brushes

Wash a celery stalk very well and cut in half lengthways. Cut into 3 in/8cm lengths. Using a sharp knife make cuts along the length of the celery, leaving about ½ in/ 1.76 cm at one end intact. Drop into iced water for a few hours to open out and curl.

FRUIT

Citrus Butterflies

Cut the citrus fruit into thin slices crossways and divide each slice into four, making four even-sized triangles. Make each wing by positioning the points of two triangles together and place two very fine strips of red pepper, to represent the feelers, in the centre.

Citrus Swans

Thinly slice the citrus fruit crossways and cut each slice in half. Separate the peel from the flesh by making a cut along the edge of the slice leaving only ¼ in/1 cm connected at one end. Bend the cut peel backwards and tuck into the fruit slice.

Citrus Twists

Thinly slice the citrus fruit and make a cut from the centre to one of the outer edges. Hold the slice of fruit in both hands with your fingers placed on either side of the cut and gently twist in opposite directions.

Citrus Wings

Make two small diagonal cuts in the centre of the unpeeled fruit, working from top to bottom and angling the knife so that you obtain a wedge. Remove the wedge and keep for later. Cut three more wedges out of the fruit following the same angle as the first – each wedge will be larger than the previous one. Repeat this process, working around the fruit, until you have enough wings.

Starfruit
Simply slice the starfruit thinly to enhance its natural, attractive shape.

Strawberry Fans
Only use firm, ripe strawberries for this garnish. Simply cut thin slices from just beneath the hull of the strawberry to the bottom. Gently spread the fan slices out. Place a mint sprig at the hull end of the strawberry.

Citrus Zest
Using a utensil called a 'zester' take the zest from citrus fruits such as lemons, limes, oranges, grapefruit and tangerines.

Mango, Melon, or Apple Balls
Peel the apple, melon or mango and, using a utensil known as a 'fruit baller', cut into the flesh of the fruit making small balls. You can buy different sizes of 'fruit ballers' from catering shops and good supermarkets.

BREAD

Melba Toast
Toast some ready-sliced bread and trim off the crusts. Using a very sharp knife, split each slice in half through the middle – giving you two slices from every one slice. Toast the cut side gently until it turns golden brown and curls up. Once cooled it can be stored in an airtight tin.

Croûtons
Toast some thickly sliced bread and cut into different shapes – cubes, hearts, triangles, circles, for example.

PASTRY

Pastry Flower

Roll out a thin piece of pastry, about 1½ in/4 cm wide and 5 in/13 cm long. Make a 'fringe' by making regular cuts three-quarters of the way across the pastry strip. Roll out the pastry around the end of a teaspoon or skewer. Remove the teaspoon and open out the 'petals'. Chill for 30 minutes before cooking in a hot oven.

Pastry Shapes

Use small pastry or biscuit cutters to cut out interesting shapes from the pastry. Teddy bears, hearts, crescents or diamonds all look attractive as a garnish.

CHAPTER SEVEN

The Ingredients and the Recipes

The recipes you will find in this book are all good for us in as much as they are low in fat, low in cholesterol, low in sugar and salt while being high in fibre. They reflect recent thinking and research on what constitutes a healthy diet.

Most of the ingredients I use you will be familiar with but there may be one or two that you have not used before. Tofu, for example, is a soya bean curd that is a good substitute for cream. Some supermarkets do stock it but if you have difficulty finding it then try your local health shop. Low-sodium baking powder, unhydrogenated margarine, concentrated soya milk and sugar-free soya milk can all be purchased easily from a good health shop.

INGREDIENTS TO AVOID OR MINIMIZE	WHY?	HEALTHIER ALTERNATIVES
All red meats	High in fat, especially saturated type, cholesterol and calories	White meat (except duck and goose), fish and beans and pulses
Duck and goose	High fat content, especially saturated and cholesterol	Chicken, turkey, pigeon
Gravies made from meat juices	High fat content, especially saturated type, cholesterol and calories	Vegetable-based gravies or gravies with the fat skimmed off
Stock cubes	High salt content	Home-made stock or low-salt varieties

INGREDIENTS TO AVOID OR MINIMIZE	WHY?	HEALTHIER ALTERNATIVES
Processed meats, i.e. sausages, burgers, luncheon meats	High fat, especially saturated type, cholesterol, salt and calories	Home-made using low-fat ingredients or low-fat, low-salt varieties
Mayonnaise, salad creams and salad dressings	High fat content, especially saturated, cholesterol and calories	Low-calorie and low-fat varieties
Tomato ketchups, pickles and sauces	High sugar and salt content	Reduced sugar and salt varieties
Dairy cream – all types	High saturated fat, cholesterol and calories (double cream is 48 per cent fat)	Low-fat natural yogurt, fromage frais, Greek strained yogurt and tofu
Non-dairy cream substitutes	High in saturated fat and calories	Low-fat natural yogurt, fromage frais, Greek strained yogurt and tofu
Commercial dairy and non-dairy ice-cream	High in saturated fat and calories	Home-made ice-cream using healthy ingredients, low-calorie yogurt ice-creams, and soya ice-creams
Egg yolks	High in saturated fat and cholesterol	Extra egg whites
Full cream milk	High in saturated fat and cholesterol	Skimmed, semi-skimmed milk or sugar-free soya milk

Ingredients to Avoid or Minimize	Why?	Healthier Alternatives
Evaporated or condensed milk	High in saturated fat, cholesterol, sugar and calories	Reduced fat and sugar varieties, concentrated soya milk, tofu, fromage frais and low-fat yogurt
Full-fat natural yogurt	High in saturated fat	Low-fat natural yogurt
Fruit-flavoured yogurt	High in saturated fat, sugar and calories	Low-fat natural yogurt blended with fresh fruit
Full-fat cream and soft cheeses	High in saturated fat, cholesterol and calories	Low-fat soft and cream cheese, quark, cottage cheese and Ricotta cheese
Hard cheeses	High in saturated fat, cholesterol and calories	Low, or half-fat varieties available – e.g. Edam and Gouda
Butter	High in saturated fat, cholesterol and calories	Unhydrogenated polyunsaturated margarine, low-fat spreads
Suet	High in saturated fat, cholesterol and calories	Unhydrogenated polyunsaturated margarine, low-fat cooking spread and oils.
Lard	High in saturated fat, cholesterol and calories	Unhydrogenated polyunsaturated margarine, low-fat cooking spread and oils

INGREDIENTS TO AVOID OR MINIMIZE	WHY?	HEALTHIER ALTERNATIVES
Hydrogenated margarines	High in saturated fat, cholesterol and calories	Unhydrogenated polyunsaturated margarines and low-fat spreads
Blended margarines	High in saturated fat, cholesterol and calories	Unhydrogenated polyunsaturated margarines and low-fat spreads
Coconut oil, blended oils, Paton oil and vegetable oils	High in saturated fat	Safflower oil, sunflower oil, olive oil, low-fat oils, soya bean oil and sesame oil
Chocolate	High in saturated fat, cholesterol, sugar and calories	Carob chocolate
Cocoa powder	High in saturated fat, cholesterol, sugar and calories	Carob powder
Sugar, all types	Empty calories	Fruit juices, concentrated fruit juices, fresh fruit, dried fruit, sweet cicely, angelica, cinnamon and honey
Canned fruit in syrup	High in sugar and calories	Fresh fruit or fruit canned in own juices
Pie fillings	High in sugar and calories	Fresh and dried fruit
Sugared cereals	High in sugar, salt and calories	Sugar- and salt-free cereals

Ingredients to Avoid or Minimize	Why?	Healthier Alternatives
Biscuits	High in saturated fat, cholesterol, sugar and calories	Home-made biscuits, wholewheat cereal biscuits low in sugar, oatcakes
Commercially baked goods	High in saturated fat, cholesterol, sugar and calories	Home-made using healthy ingredients
Coconut, brazil nuts, cashew nuts	High in saturated fat (coconut is about 66 per cent)	Sunflower, pumpkin, sesame seeds, walnuts and almonds
Refined flours, e.g. white	Low in fibre	Wholemeal, granary, rye, buckwheat, mixed grain, soya and malted granary flour
Self-raising flour	High sodium content	Plain flour plus low-sodium baking powder
Baking powder	High sodium content	Low-sodium baking powder
Salt	High sodium content	Low-sodium salt, herbs and spices
Pastry	High in fat, especially saturated, cholesterol and calories	Filo pastry or low-fat pastry
Refined pastas and rice	Low in fibre	Unrefined wholewheat varieties
Jams and jellies	High sugar and calorie content	Low-sugar varieties and sugar-free varieties

Each of the recipes contains a row of symbols to tell you, at a glance, about the number of servings and whether it can be frozen. The key to the symbols is:

F   Suitable for freezing   4   Number of servings

The ingredients are given in both imperial and metric – please only use one *or* the other and *not* both. (I don't know about you but I am still not metricated; my brain thinks only in pounds and ounces.)

MEASUREMENT EQUIVALENTS

Grams (g)	Ounces (oz)	Millilitres (ml)	Fluid Ounces (fl oz)
25	1	25	1
40	1½	50	2
50	2	75	3
60	2½	125	4
75	3	150	5 (¼ pint)
100	4	175	6
125	4	200	7
150	5	225	8
175	6	250	10 (½ pint)
200	7	275	10 (½ pint)
225	8 (½ lb)	300	11
250	9	350	12
275	10	375	13
300	11	400	15 (¾ pint)
350	12	425	16 (¾ pint)
375	13	450	17
400	14	475	18
425	15	500	20 (1 pint)
450	16 (1 lb)	550	20 (1 pint)
475	17		
500	18	850	30
700	24 (1½ lb)	1 litre	35
1000 (1 kg)	2 pounds	1.2 litres	40 (2 pints)

The tablespoons and teaspoons used in my recipes are the standard sizes of 15 ml and 5 ml respectively, and should be level, not heaped.

CENTIMETRES TO INCHES

Centimetres	Inches
0.6	¼
1	½
2.5	1
5	2
7.5	3
10	4
12.5	5
15	6
18	7
20	8
23	9
25	10
28	11
30	12

OVEN TEMPERATURES

Temperature	Centigrade (C)	Fahrenheit (F)	Gas Mark (GM)
	70	150	
	80	175	
	100	200	
Very cool	110	225	¼
	120	250	½
	140	275	1
Cool	150	300	2
Warm	160	325	3
	180	350	4
Fairly hot	190	375	5
	200	400	6
	220	425	7
Hot	230	450	8
Very hot	240	475	9
	260	500	9

Just a quick word on oven temperatures. Ovens can vary enormously and you will probably know whether yours runs hotter or cooler than it should. The temperatures given in the recipes should therefore be used only as a guide. If you know your oven to be hot then reduce the temperature accordingly. The reverse is also true if your oven is cooler.

NORTH AMERICAN MEASUREMENT EQUIVALENTS

1 pt/550 ml	water	2¼ cups
1 oz/25 g	margarine	2 tbsp
1 oz/25 g	flour	2 tbsp
1 oz/25 g	chopped seeds	2 tbsp
1 oz/25 g	grated cheese	4 tbsp
1 lb/450 g	breadcrumbs	8 cups
1 lb/450 g	rice (uncooked)	2 cups
1 lb/450 g	wholemeal flour	4 cups
1 lb/450 g	mashed potato	2 cups
1 lb/450 g	small beans	2 cups
1 lb/450 g	large beans	3 cups
1 lb/450 g	ground seeds	4 cups
1 lb/450 g	cottage cheese	2 cups
1 lb/450 g	soft cheese	2 cups

CHAPTER EIGHT

A Fine Romance

I must admit that I am an incurable romantic. Romantic to the point of being positively soppy in fact. And funnily enough it has made it very difficult for me to write this particular chapter. I've had to restrain myself from going over the top and making everything in the shape of hearts and giving all the dishes romantic names. I am the one in a cinema who always cries at the sad and happy parts of the film – there isn't much hope for me, is there? Thank goodness for waterproof mascara!

An ex-manager of mine told me a lovely story about a newly engaged couple who were entertaining both sets of parents and wanted to make a good impression. He was the cook and so volunteered to make the main course and dessert. His fiancée was given the task of preparing the starter – melon and prawns in port. So far so good. The evening prior to the gathering it was suggested, politely, that the melon should really be marinated overnight. She duly disappeared into the kitchen. Two hours before the dinner was due to start, one of the guests ventured into the kitchen for some ice cubes and quickly returned to the others asking, 'What's that washing-up bowl doing in the fridge with a melon in it?' Upon investigation it came to light that a full bottle of port had been poured into the bowl and a whole, untouched melon just plopped in to marinate! It hadn't even been skinned, let alone chopped. Never mind, you live and learn, don't you?

Talking about marinating fruit, I must tell you something that happened to me a few years ago. I spent one afternoon this particular summer marinating peaches, ten pounds of them, in brandy. That evening some friends popped in for drinks and Richard offered Rémy Martin. Unfortunately, their response was positive. Unfortunate because I had used two full bottles of Rémy for my peaches. I then rubbed salt in the wound by enthusiastically saying that I hadn't touched the two-star Metaxa we had brought from Greece. The air was blue for quite a while. Not being a brandy drinker I didn't know the difference – an easy mistake to make. That's my excuse anyway and I'm sticking to it. You'll be glad to know that the peaches tasted superb!

BACK TO BASICS

Good planning and preparation are more important for a romantic meal than for any other occasion if for only one reason: you don't want to spend most of the time in the kitchen on your own, do you? After all, that wouldn't be very romantic! Ideally the meal should look and taste impressive and yet not require lots of last-minute preparation. Avoid temperamental dishes such as soufflés and difficult sauces. It's also a good idea to plan at least one course that can be prepared well in advance and even frozen. This mini-mizes any last-minute hiccups and ensures the time is spent where it should be – with your loved one.

One area of constant confusion about any dinner party is how many courses there should be. Quite honestly, I feel that you can easily overdo this by serving too many courses. There is nothing more embarrassing than guests being too full to eat the final course of a meal and yet feeling obliged to try and force it down. I know that there is a certain snobbery associated with meals of five-plus courses. The usual number, however, in this country is three or four consisting of a starter, main course, dessert and maybe cheese. If you wish you can add a fish course after the starter followed by a sorbet to refresh the palate for the main course. Remember that not only does it take time to prepare these extra courses but also to eat them. So do allow plenty of time and give at least ten minutes between courses for the food to settle a little. You can also work the other way and have just two courses for your dinner. It's all up to you really.

I always tend to choose the main course first and then work the other courses in around it, taking into account the textures, colours and heaviness of the dishes. I would never, for example, serve pastry twice in one meal because it's just too filling. A good piece of sound advice is not to serve very spicy food unless you know your guests well enough to be aware of their tastes. The same thing goes for high-fibre food. I once made the mistake of serving a fairly high-fibre meal to Richard's brother and girlfriend who were staying with us for a romantic weekend. Bryan spent the weekend in bed with bad stomach cramps – he wasn't used to high-fibre food apparently. I've heard of more romantic ways to spend time together.

Try and organize yourself by making lists of what to buy, what to do and when to do it. As you complete each task cross it off the schedule – it really does help. If you can plan to have *everything* prepared a couple of hours before the guests are due to arrive, that takes the pressure off you.

When it comes to the coffee and liqueurs I tend to move everyone into the lounge, but again there are no set rules. I prefer it because it tends to spark conversations off again, which may have started to flag at the table and also the seating tends to be more comfortable and informal.

The atmosphere you create for a romantic meal is important as it sets the mood. I like soft, muted lighting and so candles are placed on the dining table, window-sills, coffee tables – anywhere in fact. Candles look especially nice when they are reflected in a mirror or pane of glass. Candlelight is also far more flattering to the face than the harsh glare of electric lighting – which is the main reason I use candles! Nice, easy-to-listen-to music in the background is essential – not too loud and not boppy. Pot pourri in cups, saucers, bowls and glasses imparts the most beautiful and yet subtle fragrances to any room. Choose a different type for each room to add interest.

With all that working for you how can it fail!

ENGAGEMENT MEAL
FOR EIGHT

Menu

ASPARAGUS AND CHEESE SOUP
WITH
POPPY SEED AND LEMON ROLLS

FISH WELLINGTON
WITH
POTATO AND ALMOND CROQUETTES
CARROTS WITH SULTANAS
BROCCOLI IN LEMON

PASHKA

COFFEE OR TEA
WITH
NIBBLES OF FRESH FRUIT

Asparagus and Cheese Soup

(F 8)

PREPARATION TIME: 10 minutes
COOKING TIME: 10 minutes

INGREDIENTS:
3 10 oz/275 g tins asparagus
1 lb/450 g potatoes, cooked
8 tbsp silken tofu
1 pt/550 ml skimmed milk
2 pt/1.2 l vegetable stock
4 oz/100 g low-fat cheese, grated
black pepper and low-sodium salt

METHOD
1 Put the asparagus, plus the juice, potatoes, tofu and milk into a liquidizer and blend until smooth.
2 Pour this mixture into a saucepan with the vegetable stock and heat gently. Add the grated cheese, season and serve. Serve with warm poppy seed and lemon rolls.

Poppy Seed and Lemon Rolls

(F 8)

PREPARATION TIME: 20 minutes
COOKING TIME: 12 minutes
TEMPERATURE: 230°C/450°F/Gas 7

INGREDIENTS:
4 oz/100 g plain wholemeal flour
4 oz/100 g plain white flour
3 tsp low-sodium baking powder
2 oz/50 g low-fat cooking spread
2 tbsp poppy seeds
2 lemons, zest of
6 tbsp skimmed milk

METHOD

1 Sift the flours and baking powder and rub in the low-fat spread until the mixture resembles fine breadcrumbs.
2 Add the poppy seeds and lemon zest. Stir in enough milk to give a soft dough.
3 Form the dough into 8 balls and place on a greased baking sheet. Brush with milk and cook until golden brown.

Fish Wellington

(F 8)

PREPARATION TIME: 20 minutes
COOKING TIME: 25 minutes
TEMPERATURE: 220°C/425°F/Gas 7

INGREDIENTS:
1 onion, peeled and finely chopped
4 oz/125 g mushrooms, wiped and chopped
1 tbsp extra virgin olive oil
6 oz/175 g vegetable pâté
4 tbsp fromage frais
black pepper and low-sodium salt
8 filo pastry sheets
1 tbsp walnut oil
2 large fillets of haddock, skinned

METHOD

1 Fry the onion and mushrooms in the olive oil for 2 minutes. Remove from the heat.
2 Mash the vegetable pâté with the fromage frais, onion and mushrooms. Season to taste.
3 Lightly oil each filo sheet with the walnut oil and place one on top of the other.
4 Lay one haddock fillet in the centre of the filo and spread the stuffing mixture over it. Top with the other haddock fillet.
5 Carefully, gather up the filo pastry to encase the fish, sealing it along the top and at both ends. Lightly brush with oil.

6   Place on a baking sheet and bake for about 25 minutes until the fish is cooked through.
7   Serve hot, garnished with lemon twists and parsley.

Potato and Almond Croquettes
(F 8)

PREPARATION TIME: 10 minutes
COOKING TIME: 30 minutes
TEMPERATURE: 200°C/400°F/Gas 6

INGREDIENTS:
2 lb/900 g potatoes, boiled
2 oz/50 g low-fat cooking spread
6 tbsp skimmed milk, approximately
2 oz/50 g ground almonds
black pepper and low-sodium salt
2 oz/50 g flaked almonds

METHOD
1   Mash the potatoes with the low-fat spread and enough milk to make a light, firm mixture.
2   Add the ground almonds and season.
3   Form the mixture into 16 ball shapes.
4   Roll the balls in the flaked almonds and place on a lightly oiled baking tray. Cook until golden brown.

Carrots with Sultanas

(F 8)

PREPARATION TIME: 5 minutes
COOKING TIME: 25 minutes

INGREDIENTS:
8 carrots, scrubbed
2 oz/50 g sultanas

METHOD
1 Cut the carrots into long thin strips and steam for 20 minutes, until just tender.
2 Add the sultanas and cook for a further 5 minutes. Serve hot.

Broccoli with Lemon

(F 8)

PREPARATION TIME: 5 minutes
COOKING TIME: 10 minutes

INGREDIENTS:
1½ lb/700 g broccoli, trimmed and cut into florets
2 oz/50 g low-fat cooking spread
8 fl oz/225 ml vegetable stock
4 tsp cornflour
3 tbsp lemon juice plus zest

METHOD
1 Steam the broccoli until just tender.
2 Meanwhile, melt the low-fat spread in the stock and bring to the boil gently.
3 Blend the cornflour with the lemon juice until smooth. Add to the pan along with the lemon zest.
4 Bring back to the boil and simmer until it thickens and becomes glossy.
5 Arrange the broccoli in a serving dish and pour on the lemon sauce. Serve hot.

Pashka

(F 8)

PREPARATION TIME: 15 minutes
CHILLING TIME: Overnight

INGREDIENTS:
1 lb/450 g low-fat soft cheese
2 lemons, zest of
1 tbsp lemon juice
2 oz/50 g sugar
4 tbsp fromage frais
2 oz/50 g fresh raspberries
2 oz/50 g raisins
2 oz/50 g blanched almonds, toasted
1 oz/25 g flaked almonds, toasted

METHOD
1   Beat together the low-fat soft cheese, lemon zest, juice and sugar. Stir in the fromage frais, raspberries, raisins and blanched almonds.
2   Line a 1 l/1¾ pt pudding basin with a piece of muslin, leaving enough hanging over the sides to cover the top.
3   Spoon in the mixture and cover with the muslin. Place a saucer with a 1 lb/450 g weight on top of the basin and leave overnight.
4   To serve, unfold the muslin, and invert the pudding on to a serving plate. Remove the muslin and decorate with almonds.

ST VALENTINE'S DINNER FOR TWO

Menu

**MONKFISH AND PRAWN RAMEKINS
WITH
ASPARAGUS SAUCE**

**STUFFED CHICKEN BREASTS
WITH
SPICED POTATOES
ENDIVE DELIGHT**

PASSION AND BANANA SURPRISE

COFFEE OR TEA

Monkfish and Prawn Ramekins
(2)

PREPARATION TIME: 20 minutes
COOKING TIME: 20 minutes
CHILLING TIME: 1 hour
TEMPERATURE: 180°C/350°F/Gas 4

INGREDIENTS:
8 spinach or lettuce leaves, blanched
2 oz/50 g prawns
1 tbsp fresh dill, chopped
4 oz/100 g monkfish
1 egg white
¼ pt/150 ml fromage frais
1 tbsp lemon juice
black pepper and low-sodium salt
2 oz/50 g salmon, cooked
2 king prawns

ASPARAGUS SAUCE:
2 oz/50 g tinned asparagus
1 tbsp fromage frais
a little asparagus juice to thin the sauce

METHOD
1 Lightly oil 2 individual heart-shaped tins or ramekins. Remove the stalks from the spinach leaves and use them or the lettuce to line the base and sides of the tins – remember to leave some for the top.
2 Mix the prawns with the dill.
3 Cut the monkfish into pieces and purée until smooth. Add the egg white, fromage frais, lemon juice and seasoning.
4 Pour half the monkfish purée into the base of the ramekins. Cover with the prawns.
5 Spoon the remaining monkfish mixture into the tins followed by the salmon.
6 Use the remaining spinach leaves to cover and seal the top. Cover tightly with greased foil and place the ramekins in a

dish that has enough hot water to come halfway up their sides.
7 Cook for about 25 minutes or until firm to the touch. Chill until required.
8 To make the sauce, place all the ingredients in a food processor or liquidizer and blend until smooth. Chill until required.
9 Turn out and serve the ramekins with the asparagus sauce and garnish with a king prawn and lemon wings.

Stuffed Chicken Breasts

(F 2)

PREPARATION TIME: 20 minutes
COOKING TIME: 30 minutes
TEMPERATURE: 200°C/400°F/Gas 6

INGREDIENTS:
1 tbsp extra virgin olive oil
½ onion, peeled and chopped
2 garlic cloves, crushed
2 oz/50 g sunflower seeds
½ red pepper, seeded and finely chopped
2 oz/50 g wholemeal breadcrumbs
black pepper and low-sodium salt
1 piece stem ginger, chopped finely
2 oz/50 g low-fat cheese, grated
2 chicken breasts, skinned
¼ pt/150 ml dry white wine

SAUCE:
low-fat cooking spread
2 oz/50 g almonds, slivered
½ orange pepper, seeded and chopped
½ onion, peeled and chopped
½ oz/15 g wholemeal flour
¼ pt/150 ml chicken stock
black pepper and low-sodium salt
3 tbsp silken tofu, liquidized

METHOD

1   To make the stuffing first heat the olive oil and fry the onion, garlic, sunflower seeds and pepper for about 3 minutes.

2   Add the breadcrumbs, seasoning, ginger and cheese. Mix well.

3   Make slits along the chicken breasts to form pockets for the stuffing. Divide the stuffing between the chicken breasts, pressing in firmly.

4   Place the chicken breasts with the wine in a covered ovenproof dish and cook for about 30 minutes.

5   Then make the sauce by melting the low-fat cooking spread and frying the almonds until brown. Add the orange pepper and onion and fry until fairly soft. Remove. Add the flour to the pan and cook for 1 minute. Add the stock and seasoning.

6   Return the almond and pepper mixture to the pan along with the strained juices from the cooked chicken breasts. Bring to the boil and add the tofu.

7   Pour the sauce around the breasts of chicken and serve.

Spiced Potatoes

(2)

PREPARATION TIME: 10 minutes
COOKING TIME: 20 minutes

INGREDIENTS:
4 potatoes, medium size, well scrubbed
½ oz/15 g low-fat cooking spread
1 tbsp extra virgin olive oil
1 tsp ground cumin
1 tsp cumin seeds
1 onion, peeled and finely chopped

METHOD

1 Parboil the potatoes in salted water for 10 minutes before cutting into thin slices. Pat dry with kitchen roll.
2 Heat the cooking spread and oil and fry the ground cumin and cumin seeds for 1 minute, stirring continuously.
3 Add the onion and fry for a further minute before adding the sliced potatoes. Cook until the potatoes are brown on both sides.
4 Drain off any excess fat and pat with kitchen roll.

Endive Delight

(2)

PREPARATION TIME: 10 minutes

INGREDIENTS:
6 endive leaves, washed and dried
2 spring onions, washed and chopped
½ fennel bulb, sliced thinly
6 spinach leaves, washed and dried

METHOD
Mix all the ingredients together.

Passion and Banana Surprise

(2)

PREPARATION TIME: 5 minutes

INGREDIENTS:
2 passion fruit
1 banana, ripe
2 tsp lemon juice
1 tsp lemon zest
2 tbsp Greek strained yogurt

METHOD

1 Cut the passion fruit in half and scoop out the flesh.
2 Mash the banana with the lemon juice. Add the lemon zest and passion fruit, and fold in the yogurt.
3 Spoon the mixture into 2 stemmed glasses and garnish with an edible flower such as primrose or nasturtium.

WEDDING ANNIVERSARY BREAKFAST

Menu

GRANOLA CRUNCH
WITH
YOGURT

DEVILLED MUSHROOMS
WITH
CHAMPAGNE

FRESH FRUIT SALAD

COFFEE OR TEA

Granola Crunch

(10)

PREPARATION TIME: 25 minutes
COOKING TIME: 30 minutes
TEMPERATURE: 160°C/325°F/Gas 3

INGREDIENTS:
5 tbsp clear honey
4 oz/100 g jumbo oats
4 oz/100 g barley oats
4 oz/100 g bran oats
1 lemon, zest of
1 orange, zest of
1 grapefruit, zest of
1 tsp vanilla essence
2 tbsp sunflower seeds
2 tbsp pumpkin seeds
3 oz/75 g dried prunes, chopped finely
3 oz/75 g dried apricots, chopped finely
3 oz/75 g dried apple, chopped finely

METHOD

1   Heat the honey and stir in the cereals, zest, vanilla essence and seeds.

2   Spread the mixture on to 2 non-stick baking sheets. Bake for 25 minutes, stirring once.

3   Stir in the dried fruit and leave to cool. Store in an airtight container.

4   Serve with natural low-fat yogurt, skimmed milk or un-sweetened fruit juice.

Devilled Mushrooms

(2)

PREPARATION TIME: 15 minutes
COOKING TIME: 11 minutes
TEMPERATURE: 220°C/425°F/Gas 7

INGREDIENTS:
2 slices wholemeal bread 1 in/2.5 cm thick
1 oz/25 g low-fat cooking spread
2 garlic cloves, crushed
6 oz/175 g button mushrooms, wiped and trimmed
½ lemon, juice of
2 tbsp fromage frais
2 tsp low-sugar tomato ketchup
1 tsp horseradish sauce
1 tsp French mustard
1 tsp grated nutmeg
black pepper and low-sodium salt
fresh herbs for garnish

METHOD

1   Cut the bread into 2 4 in/10 cm diameter circles. Cut out a 3 in/7.5 cm diameter circle almost to the bottom and remove the centre carefully to form a case. Toast until golden brown on both sides.

2   Heat the cooking spread and sauté the garlic and mushrooms for 1 minute. Remove from the heat, add the lemon juice and pile into the bread cases. Mix the fromage frais with the remaining ingredients. Spoon over the mushrooms. Bake for about 10 minutes. Garnish with fresh herbs.

Fresh Fruit Salad

(2)

PREPARATION TIME: 5 minutes

INGREDIENTS:
1 orange, peeled and chopped
1 grapefruit, peeled and chopped
4 strawberries, washed and halved
1 kiwi fruit, sliced

METHOD

Mix all the fruits together and serve well chilled in long-stemmed glasses.

CHAPTER NINE

Party Time

THE CHILDREN'S PARTY

To be appealing to children, food must be interesting and that means plenty of different, bright colours, shapes and textures. Preparing a children's party is wonderful as it gives your imagination the chance to run riot – it's so much fun!

One of the main factors to bear in mind is that children are very resistant to foods that look different from the norm – and that makes it difficult to introduce healthier foods into their diet. Hence the reluctance of most children even to try eating wholemeal bread if they are used to white.

Yet it is important that children, like adults, cut their intake of fat, especially the saturated type, sugar and salt and increase their consumption of fibre. In fact these guidelines are more important where the diets of children are concerned because it is in these years that tastes are formed. What we eat in childhood forms the blueprint, very often, of what we eat in adulthood. Do you remember being given sweets at the doctor's for having a measles jab without screaming the whole surgery down? I certainly do! It is associations like this that explain the strong link between sugary foods and 'comfort' eating. Psychology plays an important role in our eating habits and that is especially true where children are concerned. What it boils down to is a case of playing them at their own game. Wholemeal bread, for example, will happily be eaten by children – if it is hidden. So try making pinwheel sandwiches or triangles using a mixture of white and wholemeal bread, making sure that it is the white bread on show! Interesting and colourful fillings could include low-fat soft cheese mixed with chopped prawns or watercress: red lentil with tomato; Gouda cheese with tomato purée and garlic – the variations are endless.

And, the party favourite – a jelly. Well, I have to tell you that a jelly is a jelly, is a jelly. So make it with fresh fruit juice instead of the 'normal' sugar and chemical-laden varieties. It looks virtually the same, is much healthier and it tastes better. Instead of giving your children sugary soft drinks, why not try fresh fruit juice diluted with carbonated mineral water? And low-fat yogurt blended with any combination of fresh fruit and skimmed milk is a real winner – you could also add a scoop of low-fat ice-cream. Don't forget the magic touch though – big, colourful bendy straws and lots of ice.

Healthy eating, whether it be for children or adults, is all about practicality – so compromise a little! Even the infamous chip can be made healthier by cutting the potato into 'thick' chips, not using crinkle cuts, frying in olive oil and patting dry on kitchen roll. Enjoy the party!

BACK TO BASICS

Children's parties are definitely fun, but they are also demanding and exhausting. Be warned! For your own sake, don't invite too many children as they do require quite a bit of supervision and the children themselves can feel a little overpowered too. Okay, now the difficult part – how many is too many? It's like asking how long is a piece of string, but as a guideline try inviting six children for a child about three years old; about twelve for a six-year-old and then after that age play it by ear, because a lot will depend on the class size at school. What a thought! Never be tempted to mix age groups at a children's party, it just does not work. What keeps a three-year-old happy and occupied will bore the pants off a six-year-old and that is a recipe for disaster (excuse the pun!).

A children's party tends to be more successful if you use two rooms – one for feeding and one for playing. This also reduces the risk of accidents. Talking of which, remove anything breakable and lock all furniture where possible. It's a good idea to take keys out of doors, especially the bathroom. The last thing you want is for a child to be locked in the toilet – although I don't know, it might be a good idea in some cases! Do make sure that all chemicals and medicines are out of sight and out of reach of the children. And have plenty of kitchen roll at the ready for those all too frequent spillages.

For those still brave enough to hold a children's party, you must consider the entertainment. If you can pull white rabbits from a top hat and make coins appear from behind a child's ear, then fine. Otherwise, why not consider engaging a magician for at least part of the time. Don't leave things to happen by chance – all the games must be planned and organized. Children of any age like to be active so try to keep them busy. An incentive for games to go well is to introduce an element of competition with small prizes for the 'winners'.

Or why not organize a fancy dress competition? I'm really into these. You can tell because a couple of years ago the landlord of my local 'posh' pub asked if I wanted to buy tickets for a fancy dress dinner dance. Eagerly I said 'Yes', and bought ten tickets. Just up my street, I thought. I organized good friends into joining in the spirit of things. And didn't they just! Two friends turned up as clowns with all the make-up, noses, luminous hair, bright baggy clothes – the lot. Some wore period costume. One very good friend, Melvyn, went all Elizabethan and wore stockings and those Edmund of *Blackadder*-type clothes. What a sight his legs were. And that hat! Richard and I went as aristocratic tramps with torn, dirty and ragged dinner suits, top hats with holes in and bare feet. You get the idea, don't you? We all arrived at the pub, except for the clowns who were late, and the whole place went deathly quiet. You could hear a pin drop as people stopped chattering, eating and drinking to look at us. There wasn't a fancy dress party at all. I'd been conned. The clowns arrived to the same response and didn't talk to me for three months! It was a good evening and we all took it in good part. We were awarded a bottle of champagne and we were the talking point of the night – and for some months thereafter!

THE CHILDREN'S PARTY

Menu

ANIMAL, SHIP AND PINWHEEL SANDWICHES
MUSHROOM BURGERS
CHEESE AND TOMATO WHIRLS

BIRTHDAY CAKE
FRESH FRUIT JELLIES
JELLY SNOW
CAROB CUPS
ORANGE AND CURRANT BISCUITS

ORANGE FLIP
STRAWBERRY CRUSH
BANANARAMA

Animal Sandwiches

(24)

PREPARATION TIME: 10 minutes

INGREDIENTS:
12 slices wholemeal bread
12 slices white bread
low-fat spread
4 oz/100 g tuna in brine, drained
1 tbsp low-calorie mayonnaise
few drops vinegar

METHOD
1 Butter the slices of bread with the low-fat spread.
2 Mix together the tuna, mayonnaise and vinegar and mash well.
3 Spread the tuna on to the slices of wholemeal bread and sandwich the white slices on top.
4 Using an animal cutter, such as a bear or duck, cut two shapes from each sandwich.
5 Cover with clingfilm until required.

Ship Sandwiches

(12)

PREPARATION TIME: 10 minutes

INGREDIENTS:
6 wholemeal bridge or finger rolls
low-fat spread
1 tbsp crunchy peanut butter
12 cocktail sticks
6 slices low-fat cheese squares, cut into 2 triangles
12 coloured triangles for flags
1 bunch watercress, washed
6 tomatoes, washed and sliced

ENGAGEMENT MEAL
Clockwise from top: Potato and Almond Croquettes, Broccoli in Lemon,
Fish Wellington and Carrots with Sultanas, Fish Wellington.

WEDDING ANNIVERSARY BREAKFAST
Right: Granola Crunch, *left:* Devilled Mushrooms.

CHILDREN'S PARTY
Fresh Fruit Jellies, Birthday Cake, Ship, Animal and Pinwheel Sandwiches,
Strawberry Crush, Bananarama and Orange Flip.

TEA PARTY
Left: Cheese Twists, *right:* Strawberry Cups.

DRINKS PARTY
Clockwise from top: Cheese Balls, Stuffed Dates and Filo Rolls, Savoury
Tartlets and Savoury Boats, Canapés, Crudités with Watercress Dip.

CHRISTMAS DAY DINNER
Clockwise from left: Festive Loaf, Christmas Pudding, Stuffed Boned Chicken
with Sautéed Potatoes, Carrots with Lemon.

BARBECUE
Clockwise from left: baked potatoes, Chilli Sauce, Fruit Kebabs, Vegetable
Kebabs, Monkfish Kebabs on a bed of wild rice.

GARDEN PARTY
From left to right: (back row) Chilled Fennel Soup, Cheese and Fennel
Terrine; (middle row) Cucumber and Cheese Ring, Tipsy Fruit Salad;
(front row) Spiced Chicken Pie, Rice Salad.

METHOD

1   Split the bridge rolls in half lengthways and butter each half with the low-fat spread, and lightly with the peanut butter.

2   To make the sails, thread a cocktail stick through the centre of each cheese triangle to form a mast. Leave ½ in/15 mm of the cocktail stick showing at the base of the triangle. Stick the base of the mast into each bread roll.

3   Attack a coloured flag to each cocktail stick top to add that finishing touch. Serve on a sea of watercress and sliced tomato.

Pinwheel Sandwiches

(F 24)

PREPARATION TIME: 10 minutes

INGREDIENTS:
4 slices wholemeal bread, crusts removed
4 slices white bread, crusts removed
1 tbsp low-fat spread
2 oz/50 g low-fat soft cheese
2 tsp tomato purée
2 oz/50 g low-fat hard cheese, grated
1 tbsp low-calorie mayonnaise

METHOD

1   Flatten each slice of bread slightly with a rolling pin and spread each with the low-fat spread.

2   Mix together the low-fat soft cheese and the tomato purée and spread on to the slices of white bread.

3   Place one slice of wholemeal bread on top of each white slice.

4   Mix together the grated cheese and mayonnaise and spread thinly on to the wholemeal bread.

5   Roll up as you would a Swiss roll and slice each roll into 6 rounds. Wrap in clingfilm until required.

Mushroom Burgers
(F 12)

PREPARATION TIME: 20 minutes
COOKING TIME: 20 minutes

INGREDIENTS:
2 tbsp olive oil
1 onion, peeled and chopped
8 oz/225 g mushrooms, wiped and sliced
2 oz/50 g wholemeal flour
¼ pt/150 ml water
1 tsp vegetable concentrate
nutmeg
4 oz/100 g wholemeal breadcrumbs
black pepper

TO COAT:
1 egg white, beaten
4 oz/100 g wholemeal breadcrumbs

METHOD

1 Heat the oil in a saucepan and gently fry the onion for 3 minutes. Add the mushrooms and cook for 1 minute, stirring.
2 Stir in the flour. Add the water, vegetable concentrate and nutmeg. Simmer for 3 minutes.
3 Off the heat, stir in the breadcrumbs and pepper. Leave to cool.
4 With flour on your hands, shape the mixture into 12 rounds. Dip in the egg white and coat with the breadcrumbs. Grill for 5 minutes each side.
5 Serve hot or cold in wholemeal bread or baps.

Cheese and Tomato Whirls

(F 24)

PREPARATION TIME: 10 minutes
COOKING TIME: 12 minutes
TEMPERATURE: 230°C/450°F/Gas 8

INGREDIENTS:
4 oz/100 g plain wholemeal flour
4 oz/100 g plain white flour
6 oz/175 g low-fat cooking spread
6 oz/175 g low-fat hard cheese, grated
½ tsp mustard powder
1 tbsp tomato purée

METHOD

1 Put the flours into a bowl and mix in the low-fat cooking spread. Add the cheese and mustard.
2 Form into a dough and roll out on a lightly floured surface into 2 oblongs about 12 in × 10 in/30.5 cm × 25.5 cm and ¼ in/6 mm thick. Lightly spread with the tomato purée.
3 Roll up from the two narrow edges so that the rolls meet in the middle making a sort of 'B' shape. Trim off the edges and slice into 12 pieces.
4 Place cut side down on a greased baking tray, leaving enough room for them to spread.
5 Cook for about 12 minutes.

Birthday Cake
(F 12)

PREPARATION TIME: 25 minutes
COOKING TIME: 50 minutes
TEMPERATURE: 160°C/325°F/Gas 3

INGREDIENTS:
6 oz/75 g plain wholemeal flour
3 tsp low-sodium baking powder
4 oz/125 g polyunsaturated margarine, unhydrogenated
3 oz/75 g soft brown sugar
1–2 tbsp orange juice
2 egg whites
few drops natural red food colouring
few drops natural green food colouring
½ tbsp carob powder

FROSTING:
4 oz/125 g carob chocolate bar
1 tsp polyunsaturated margarine, unhydrogenated
5 tbsp fromage frais

METHOD
1   Lightly grease and line a 7 in/18 cm round cake tin.
2   Sift the flour and baking powder into a large mixing bowl. Add the margarine, sugar, orange juice and egg whites and beat well until the mixture is light and fluffy. You may need to add a little water.
3   Divide the mixture between 4 separate bowls. Add a few drops of the red food colouring to one bowl, green to another and mix the carob powder well into one of the other bowls. This gives us the 4 colours for the marble effect. Use a separate spoon for each colour.
4   Drop different colours of the cake mixture into the cake tin until the mixture is all used. Smooth the top.
5   Bake for about 50 minutes in a preheated oven. Leave to cool in the tin for a minute before removing, and tear off the lining paper. Cool on a wire rack.

6   Make the topping by melting the carob bar in a small bowl over a pan of hot water. Add the margarine and beat well. Remove from the heat and stir in the fromage frais. Leave to cool for a few minutes before covering the cake with the mixture. Decorate as you wish with candles and ribbons. Leave to cool and set a little before slicing.

You can easily make this cake into the face of a clown, the shape of a ladybird, or a hedgehog – even a train. Have fun!

Fresh Fruit Jellies

(12)

PREPARATION TIME: 5 minutes

INGREDIENTS:
1 ½ oz/11 g sachet gelatine
¼ pt/150 ml boiling water
¾ pt/400 ml unsweetened fruit juice
2 tbsp mixed fruits, chopped

METHOD
1   Sprinkle the gelatine into the boiling water and stir briskly until completely dissolved.
2   Pour the dissolved gelatine into the fruit juice and mix well. Leave to cool slightly.
3   Stir the fruit into the juice and pour the liquid into jelly moulds. Leave to set in a refrigerator before turning out.

To ring the changes, mix a low-fat, low-sugar fruit yogurt into the fruit juice and set in the same way. This results in a creamy dessert much loved by children – and it looks good for parties too!

To enhance, or change, the colour of the fruit juices you use, add a few drops of natural food colouring – the difference it makes is amazing.

Jelly Snow

(12)

PREPARATION TIME: 20 minutes
SETTING TIME: 2 hours

INGREDIENTS:
1 pkt sugar-free strawberry jelly
¼ pt/150 ml boiling water
¼ pt/150 ml cold water
6 fl oz/175 ml low-fat evaporated milk

METHOD
1   Dissolve the jelly in the boiling water before stirring in the cold water.
2   Chill in the refrigerator until almost set – about 1 hour.
3   Whisk the evaporated milk until frothy and then gradually whisk in the jelly.
4   Pour the mixture into a large mould or into 12 individual paper jelly cases.
5   Place in the refrigerator to set.

Carob Cups

(24)

PREPARATION TIME: 15 minutes
CHILLING TIME: 2 hours

INGREDIENTS:
8 oz/225 g carob bar, melted
4 oz/100 g wholewheat flakes
2 oz/50 g raisins
24 small paper bun cases

METHOD
Mix all the ingredients together and drop spoonfuls of the mixture into the cake cases. Leave in a cool place to set for about 2 hours.

Orange and Currant Biscuits

(F 24)

PREPARATION TIME: 15 minutes
COOKING TIME: 10 minutes
TEMPERATURE: 200°C/400°F/Gas 6

INGREDIENTS:
4 oz/125 g plain wholemeal flour
½ tsp low-sodium baking powder
1 tsp cinnamon
2 oz/50 g low-fat cooking spread
1 oz/25 g ground almonds
2 oz/50 g currants
1 tbsp orange juice, fresh, plus zest

METHOD

1 Sift the flour, baking powder and cinnamon into a bowl.
2 Add the low-fat cooking spread, ground almonds, currants and zest. Add enough orange juice to make a firm dough.
3 Roll the dough out, on a lightly floured surface, to a thickness of about ¼ in/6 mm and cut into rounds with a 2 in/5 cm cutter, or an animal cutter.
4 Place the biscuits on a lightly greased baking sheet and prick each with a fork.
5 Cook for 10 minutes and allow to cool on a wire rack.

Orange Flip

(makes 1½ pt/850 ml)

PREPARATION TIME: 2 minutes

INGREDIENTS:
1 ½ pt/275 ml carton concentrated orange juice
soda water or mineral water

METHOD
Mix the orange concentrate with enough soda or mineral water to make 1½ pt/850 ml. Chill and serve with plenty of colourful bendy straws.

Strawberry Crush

(makes 1½ pt/850 ml)

PREPARATION TIME: 3 minutes

INGREDIENTS:
1 pt/550 ml skimmed milk, cool
2 small cartons low-fat strawberry yogurt

METHOD
Place the ingredients in a blender and blend until smooth and frothy. Serve in chilled glasses with plenty of ice and colourful, big, bendy straws.

Bananarama

(makes 1½ pt/850 ml)

PREPARATION TIME: 3 minutes

INGREDIENTS:
1 pt/550 ml skimmed milk, cool
2 bananas, peeled and sliced
2 small cartons low-fat banana yogurt

METHOD
As Strawberry Crush, above.

THE TEA PARTY

The tea party, or afternoon tea as some call it, is not as popular today as it was in Victorian times. Most people no longer have time to spend a few hours each afternoon sipping fragrant tea and nibbling dainty sandwiches and cakes. The phenomenon of afternoon tea really took a hold in the 1800s as the evening meal was increasingly being taken later and later into the evening. Even with the introduction of luncheon to try and fill the gap between breakfast and evening meal, ladies still experienced hunger pangs mid-afternoon. Hence an institution was born: 'afternoon tea'. It was, however, the preserve of the upper classes – after all they were the ladies of leisure with the resources and personal contacts to host such an event.

The nearest thing to taking afternoon tea these days, at least for those lucky enough to live in Yorkshire, is a visit to Betty's Tea Rooms. What a treat. It's like travelling back in time to the days of Queen Victoria. The waitresses and waiters are immaculately attired in black and white with collars and cuffs starched and laundered to a crisp finish. Without exception, they all have the most innocent and angelic faces imaginable. And always so very polite. Old-fashioned tea trolleys piled high with delicious treats such as lemon cheesecake, fresh fruit tartlets and curd tarts. All are exquisitely presented on china plates and lace doilies. Antique teapots from this bygone age sit proudly on delft shelves. The Victorians really went to town on teapot designs – Father Christmas, witches, post-boxes, houses, racing cars, Dickens's characters – you name it and there is probably a teapot of it. And the choice of tea and coffee available is astonishing. I can remember a few years ago commenting on what a lovely fragrance there was in the shop. It just happened to be a fruit tea that was being weighed out for a customer. Without delay, containers were winging their way off the shelf for me to have a quick snifter at them. A good hour later the enthusiastic, and extremely knowledgeable, sales lady was still searching out exotic teas and coffees for me. I came out of Betty's knowing much more about tea and coffee than I thought possible, and a good deal poorer because I couldn't resist buying lots of different teas to try.

It's a shame that the concept of afternoon tea has declined over the years, but life is so hectic these days that it can only be an occasional treat. But then again we do tend to appreciate less frequent events, don't we, so maybe it's not a bad thing!

BACK TO BASICS

Plan the menu for afternoon tea around delicate sandwiches, crusts removed, cut into bite-sized pinwheels or triangles. Doorstop sandwiches are not really appropriate here. Delicate tartlets, biscuits, twists, slices of fruit cake and scones are ideal as they are acceptable to most people and easy to eat.

Try to prepare as much of the food as you can in advance. Most teabreads and fruit cakes keep well for several days wrapped in foil or kept in an airtight container. Scones and biscuits can be treated in the same way or frozen if preferred. Sandwiches can either be frozen or kept in the fridge but beware – avoid using watery fillings such as tomatoes as they will make the bread very soggy and unappetizing.

This is an occasion that demands your best linen tablecloth, preferably one that is heavily embroidered. I use a Victorian pillow case, beautifully scalloped with handworked embroidery, and because it isn't one of a pair I picked it up for only a couple of pounds in an antique shop! Pretty linen napkins are a must and so too are doilies. If you have a tiered cake stand then use it, as it really will show off your food beautifully. Pastry forks are useful especially if you are serving anything with a creamy filling, such as a fresh fruit tartlet. And, of course, use your best tea set. Tea never tastes as good as when served in a china cup. I know that's psychological but it still remains just as true.

THE TEA PARTY

Menu

THE NOT SO HUMBLE SANDWICH
CHEESE TWISTS
CREAM CHEESE ROUNDS

STRAWBERRY CUPS
FRESH STRAWBERRY ROUNDS
FRESH CHERRY RING
DUNDEE CAKE
GINGER, ALMOND AND ORANGE SHORTBREAD
BARM BRACK
ROCK BUNS
OATCAKES

The Not So Humble Sandwich

(F 8)

PREPARATION TIME: 10 minutes

INGREDIENTS:
8 thin slices of wholemeal of wholemeal bread
1 oz/25 g low-fat spread
6 oz/175 g smoked salmon
16 thin slices of cucumber
black pepper

METHOD

1   Remove the crusts from the bread and lightly spread each slice with the low-fat spread.
2   Divide the smoked salmon and cucumber between 4 slices of bread, sprinkle with black pepper and make a sandwich with the remaining bread.
3   Cut into dainty triangles and serve.

SANDWICH FILLING IDEAS

sardine pâté and spring onions
low-fat cream cheese with ginger
smoked salmon pâté
smoked mackerel pâté
prawns with tarragon
smoked breast of chicken
egg, cress and low-calorie mayonnaise
low-fat soft cheese with walnuts
grated Gouda with low-calorie mayonnaise
curried chicken
crab and apple
tuna with watercress and onion
turkey with chestnut purée
low-fat cream cheese with garlic
lentil pâté
hummus
crispy salad
prawn and avocado

Cheese Twists

(F 30)

PREPARATION TIME: 15 minutes
COOKING TIME: 7 minutes
TEMPERATURE: 230°C/450°F/Gas 8

INGREDIENTS:
6 oz/175 g low-fat cooking spread
4 oz/125 g plain wholemeal flour
4 oz/125 g plain white flour
6 oz/175 g low-fat hard cheese, grated
½ tsp mustard powder

METHOD
1   Mix the low-fat cooking spread and the flours together with a
    fork. Add the cheese and mustard.
2   Form the mixture into a dough and roll out to ¼ in/6 mm in
    thickness. Cut into strips about 2 in/5 cm long and ¼ in/6 mm
    wide. Twist the strips and place on a floured baking sheet.
3   Cook until golden brown. Cool on a wire rack.

Cream Cheese Rounds

(F 8)

PREPARATION TIME: 10 minutes

INGREDIENTS:
4 thin slices wholemeal bread
4 thin slices white bread
3 oz/75 g low-fat cream cheese
1 tbsp celery, grated
1 tbsp apple, grated
black pepper

METHOD
1   Remove the crusts from the bread. Mix together the
    remaining ingredients.

2   Spread the slices of bread with the cheese mixture and roll up Swiss roll-style.
3   Cut each roll into 4 and serve.

LOW-FAT PASTRY

PREPARATION TIME: 25 minutes

INGREDIENTS:
5 oz/150 g plain wholemeal flour
1 oz/25 g soya flour
½ tsp dried yeast, easy blend
pinch of vitamin C powder
1 egg white, lightly beaten
1 fl oz/25 ml sesame oil, cold pressed
6 tsp warm water

METHOD
1   Mix the flours, yeast and vitamin C in a bowl and add the egg white.
2   Mix the oil and warm water together and add to the bowl.
3   Form the dough into a ball and knead on a lightly floured work surface for about 6 or 7 minutes.
4   Leave the dough to rest in a lightly oiled polythene bag until required.

Strawberry Cups

PREPARATION TIME: 20 minutes
COOKING TIME: 15 minutes
TEMPERATURE: 190°C/375°F/Gas 5

INGREDIENTS:
½ qty low-fat pastry
¼ pt/150 ml fromage frais
8 oz/225 g fresh strawberries
3 tbsp low-sugar redcurrant jelly

METHOD

1 Roll out the pastry on a lightly floured surface and cut out circles with a 2 in/5 cm fluted cutter. Use to line lightly greased patty tins or small bun tins and prick each with a fork.
2 Bake blind for about 15 minutes. Cool on a wire tray.
3 Divide the fromage frais between the pastry cases and arrange the strawberries on top.
4 Melt the redcurrant jelly over a low heat and spoon over the tartlets.

Fresh Strawberry Rounds

(6)

PREPARATION TIME: 25 minutes
COOKING TIME: 12 minutes
TEMPERATURE: 220°C/425°F/Gas 7

INGREDIENTS:
4 oz/125 g plain white flour
4 oz/125 g plain wholemeal flour
3 tsp low-sodium baking powder
3 oz/75 g low-fat cooking spread
1 oz/25 g caster sugar
4 tbsp skimmed milk
1 egg, beaten

FILLING:
4 tbsp fromage frais
8 oz/225 g fresh strawberries, washed, hulled and sliced

METHOD

1 Sift together the flours and baking powder. Rub in the cooking spread. Add the sugar.
2 Beat the milk and egg together. Add enough to the mixture to give a softish dough – but not too sticky.
3 Knead for about 2 minutes on a lightly floured surface and roll out to about ½ in/1 cm thickness. Cut into 6 rounds with a 3½ in/8.5 cm cutter.

4   Place on a greased baking tray and brush the tops with milk. Bake until lightly golden.
5   Cool slightly on a wire tray but pull each one open with your fingers while just warm. To serve, simply sandwich the rounds together with the fromage frais and sliced strawberries.

Fresh Cherry Ring

(F 6)

PREPARATION TIME: 10 minutes
COOKING TIME: 55 minutes
TEMPERATURE: 180°C/350°F/Gas 4

INGREDIENTS:
4 oz/100 g caster sugar
6 oz/175 g low-fat cooking spread
3 eggs, beaten
7 oz/200 g plain wholemeal flour
4 tsp low-sodium baking powder
2 oz/50 g fresh cherries, washed, halved and stoned
2 tbsp sugar-free cherry preserve

METHOD
1   Line and grease an 8 in/20 cm ring tin.
2   Cream together the sugar and low-fat cooking spread until fluffy and light. Gradually beat in the eggs.
3   Sift the flour and baking powder and gently fold into the mixture. Stir in the cherries.
4   Spoon into the prepared tin and bake until the cake springs back to gentle pressure of the finger.
5   Cool on a wire rack.
6   Slice the cake through the centre horizontally and spread with the cherry conserve. Sandwich back together.

Dundee Cake
(F 12)

PREPARATION TIME: 20 minutes
COOKING TIME: 2½ hours
TEMPERATURE: 160°C/325°F/Gas 3

INGREDIENTS:
6 oz/175 g dried dates
¼ pt/150 ml orange juice, unsweetened
8 oz/225 g plain wholemeal flour
2 tsp ground cinnamon
4 tsp low-sodium baking powder
4 oz/125 g low-fat cooking spread
2 oranges, zest of
2 eggs
2 egg whites
4 oz/125 g dried apricots, finely chopped
4 oz/125 g currants
4 oz/125 g raisins
4 oz/125 g sultanas
2 oz/50 g flaked almonds

METHOD
1   Line and grease an 8 in/20 cm deep cake tin.
2   Place the dates and orange juice into a small pan and bring to the boil. Simmer until the dates are soft and pulpy – about 10 minutes – and leave to cool.
3   Sift the flour with the cinnamon and mix all the ingredients together, except 1 oz/25 g of the flaked almonds. Beat thoroughly.
4   The mixture should be soft enough to drop off the spoon quite easily. If it is too stiff, add a little more orange juice.
5   Spoon the mixture into the cake tin and sprinkle with the remaining almonds. Bake until firm to the touch. Cool on a wire rack.

Ginger, Almond and Orange Shortbread

(8)

PREPARATION TIME: 20 minutes
COOKING TIME: 40 minutes
TEMPERATURE: 180°C/350°F/Gas 4

INGREDIENTS:
4 oz/125 g plain wholemeal flour
4 oz/125 g plain white flour
3 oz/75 g ground almonds
2 oz/50 g sugar
½ tsp ground ginger
2 tsp stem ginger, chopped finely
8 oz/225 g low-fat cooking spread
2 oranges, zest of

METHOD

1   Place all the ingredients in a bowl and quickly mix together to form a firm dough.

2   Press the mixture into a 9 in/23 cm loose-bottomed flan tin and mark into 8 wedges.

3   Bake until pale golden brown. Cut into 8 wedges and leave in the tin to cool.

Barm Brack

(F 12)

PREPARATION TIME: 15 minutes
SOAKING TIME: Overnight
COOKING TIME: 1 hour 45 minutes
TEMPERATURE: 180°C/350°F/Gas 4

INGREDIENTS:
¾ pt/400 ml strong cold tea
4 oz/125 g sugar
12 oz/350 g mixed dried fruit
1 ripe banana, peeled and mashed
10 oz/275 g plain wholemeal flour
4 tsp low-sodium baking powder
1 egg

METHOD

1 Place the tea, sugar and dried fruit in a large bowl and leave, covered, overnight.
2 Mix the soaked fruit and sugar plus the liquid with the mashed banana, flour and low-sodium baking powder.
3 Add the beaten egg and mix well.
4 Spoon into a well-greased 8 /20 cm round cake tin and bake until firm to the touch.

Rock Buns

(F 16)

PREPARATION TIME: 10 minutes
COOKING TIME: 15 minutes
TEMPERATURE: 220°C/425°F/Gas 7

INGREDIENTS:
8 oz/225 g plain wholemeal flour
8 oz/225 g plain white flour
4 tsp low-sodium baking powder
2 tsp mixed spice
2 tsp ground cinnamon
8 oz/225 g low-fat cooking spread
8 oz/225 g mixed dried fruit
2 tsp lemon zest
2 oz/50 g sugar
2 eggs, beaten
3 tbsp milk

METHOD

1 Sift the flours with the baking powder, mixed spice and cinnamon.
2 Rub in the low-fat cooking spread until the mixture resembles breadcrumbs.
3 Stir in the dried fruit, lemon zest, sugar and eggs.
4 Mix together well until the consistency is firm yet holds together without crumbling. Add milk as necessary.
5 Place tablespoons of the mixture on to lightly oiled baking sheets, leaving enough room between them to spread a little.
6 Bake until firm and a lovely golden brown. Cool on a wire rack.

Oatcakes

(F 20)

PREPARATION TIME: 15 minutes
COOKING TIME: 20 minutes
TEMPERATURE: 190°C/375°F/Gas 5

INGREDIENTS:

2 oz/50 g plain wholemeal flour
2 oz/50 g plain white flour
1 tsp low-sodium baking powder
¼ tsp low-sodium salt
8 oz/225 g oatmeal
2 oz/50 g low-fat cooking spread
1 tbsp clear honey
3 fl oz/75 ml skimmed milk

METHOD

1   Sift the flours, baking powder and salt into a bowl. Add the oatmeal and rub in the low-fat cooking spread.

2   Stir in the honey and milk. The dough should be of a firm consistency.

3   Roll out the dough on a lightly floured surface to a thickness of about ⅛ in/2.5 mm. Cut into rounds with a 3 in/7.5 cm biscuit cutter.

4   Place the rounds on lightly greased baking sheets and bake until firm to the touch. Leave to cool for a minute or two on the baking sheets before transferring the biscuits to a wire tray.

THE DRINKS PARTY

Of all the drinks parties that you could give, a cheese and wine party must be the simplest of them all. That, funnily enough, is not necessarily a good thing because we can become too complacent. I have heard of cheese and wine parties which consisted of chunks of Cheddar cheese with pickles on cocktail sticks and cheap plonk to swill it down with – none of which sounds too appetizing.

Cheese and wine parties don't have to be expensive or time-consuming. Cheese can go quite a long way if you mix it with other ingredients such as vegetables, fruit and soft cheeses. This also reduces the fat content, and therefore the calories. To be perfectly honest, it's also a far more interesting way to serve cheese than simply slicing it, cubing it and then shoving a stick through it.

Nothing looks nicer than dainty canapés, dips, stuffed fruits and vegetables in bite-sized pieces that are colourful and interesting to look at – not to mention the taste of these delicious morsels. Once I start to eat this kind of food I find it difficult to stop. In fact, during the winter of 1990 I had occasion to stay in London on business for a week. The weather was cold and frosty and I was sitting in a very large winged chair in front of a roaring log fire, scribbling away with papers and books strewn everywhere. The hotel's assistant manager must have taken pity on me for he brought over a tray of beautiful canapés and a glass of sherry. The only slight problem was that I felt so very cosy and comfortable that I carried on eating the canapés and drinking the sherry. Needless to say, I didn't have any room left for the meal planned that very evening. I did enjoy the canapés though. The following evening even more canapés had been prepared – they obviously realized that I didn't just nibble politely at these dainty delicacies!

The drinks element of a party such as this can literally be anything you want it to be. I tend to have wines that are unusual in some way – and that doesn't mean they have to be expensive. Supermarket shelves quite often have wines from small vineyards, and even organic wines can be found alongside the 'regular' bottles. Interesting wines from all over the world can be quite a useful topic of conversation. Mix wine with other drinks to make a punch or a spritzer, consisting of wine and mineral water. Spirits can be provided but they are more expensive and I find that most people are quite happy with wine.

BACK TO BASICS

Drinks parties are the most flexible of all because there is nothing carved in stone regarding the food, drinks or even the time. Morning drinks parties usually take place at weekends, for obvious reasons, and start around 11.30 a.m., finishing a couple of hours later. Evening drinks parties can start anywhere from 6.30 p.m. to 8.30 p.m. So do make sure that there is plenty of food available for people to nibble, as the majority will be drinking on an empty stomach. At such get-togethers, I tend to allow eleven or twelve pieces of food for each person and it usually works out all right. Try to make the food small enough to eat in one or two bites, and don't use 'drippy' ingredients that could be awkward and messy to eat.

Arrange the food attractively on china plates and only pass around two at one time. Once the plates are about half-full replenish them – nothing looks less appetizing than a plate of nibbles that guests have fingered their way through. It's a good idea to stop offering food at least half an hour before the guests are due to leave, otherwise people will be very reluctant to go and you could wind up having to throw them out!

And now for the drinks. If you have plenty of time and don't mind the expense, you could serve spirit-based cocktails. For the majority of people, including myself, a decent wine or punch is more than acceptable. Remember to serve a variety of soft drinks for those who prefer not to partake of alcohol. Mineral water is an essential part of any drinks list – I am a little biased here because I drink it. Plenty of ice is required so start to build up a stock a couple of weeks before the party. As a guide, one bottle of wine will yield six glasses and one gallon of punch, thirty glasses. A bottle of spirit will yield thirty single measures. That's as helpful as I can be on the quantity of drink required – you know your friends' drinking habits better than I do. If they drink like fishes you will obviously need more booze than if they are only moderate drinkers. Another factor to play a part is, of course, how long the party lasts.

One thing to bear in mind is that if you buy your booze from a wine merchant, you can usually agree with them to return any unopened bottles, which is quite useful for such an occasion. Another advantage of purchasing from a wine merchant is that glasses can be hired at a very reasonable price – sometimes even free.

As with any party it is better to have too many people arrive than too few. An empty room is embarrassing, both for the host and the guests. So invite more people than you really need to allow for any cancellations. Large pieces of furniture are better moved out of the way, preferably against the walls. Anything valuable and breakable is really better kept safely out of harm's way – just in case you have guests who speak with their hands! In any case, make sure that there are plenty of drip mats, napkins, kitchen roll and damp cloths. And don't forget to have at least two corkscrews and two bottle openers tied down to a table leg or something, because they always go walkabout at parties.

DRINKS PARTY

Menu

WATERCRESS DIP
POTTED CHEESE
CHEESE BALLS
FRUIT AND CHEESE STICKS
STUFFED DATES
STUFFED PRUNES
FILO ROLLS
SAVOURY TARTLETS
SAVOURY BOATS
MANGETOUT WITH SMOKED SALMON
CANAPÉS
MELON AND CHEESE SQUARES
STUFFED CHERRY TOMATOES

Watercress Dip

(12)

PREPARATION TIME: 10 minutes
CHILLING TIME: 3 hours

INGREDIENTS:
4 oz/125 g cottage cheese
4 oz/125 g Ricotta cheese
4 tbsp Greek strained yogurt
2 garlic cloves, crushed
½ bunch watercress, washed and chopped
1 tbsp fresh chives, chopped
½ small onion, peeled and finely chopped
black pepper

METHOD
1   Beat the cheeses together and add the yogurt.
2   Stir in the garlic, watercress, chives and onion. Season with the black pepper.
3   Chill for at least 3 hours before serving with fresh vegetables and fruit.

Potted Cheese

(12)

PREPARATION TIME: 10 minutes
CHILLING TIME: 1 hour

INGREDIENTS:
3 oz/75 g low-fat spread
½ tsp nutmeg, freshly grated
black pepper
8 oz/225 g low-fat hard cheese, grated
1 tbsp dry sherry
1 tbsp skimmed milk

METHOD

1 Beat together the low-fat spread and seasonings. Slowly beat in the cheese.
2 Beat in the sherry and milk until you have a smooth mixture. Chill for 1 hour.
3 Serve with savoury biscuits and vegetables.

Cheese Balls

(25)

PREPARATION TIME: 15 minutes

INGREDIENTS:
4 oz/125 g Edam cheese, grated
4 oz/125 g low-fat hard cheese, crumbled
2 oz/50 g low-fat spread
1 tbsp spring onion, finely chopped
1 tbsp dry white wine
black pepper and nutmeg
1 oz/25 g wholemeal breadcrumbs
3 tbsp fresh parsley, finely chopped

METHOD

1 Mix the cheeses together and beat in the low-fat spread until the mixture is smooth.
2 Add the spring onion and wine. Season to taste.
3 Roll into balls about ½ in/1 cm in diameter.
4 Mix together the breadcrumbs and parsley. Roll the cheese balls in this mixture until well coated and chill before serving.

Fruit and Cheese Sticks

(30)

PREPARATION TIME: 30 minutes

INGREDIENTS:
4 oz/125 g low-fat hard cheese
15 strawberries, washed and drained
30 black grapes, washed and seeded
30 cocktail sticks

METHOD
1   Cut the cheese into 30 cubes.
2   Cut the strawberries in half.
3   Thread a strawberry, cheese cube and grape on to each cocktail stick.
4   Serve either on a plate or with the sticks pierced into an orange half or some other suitable fruit.

Stuffed Dates

(makes 30 approximately)

PREPARATION TIME: 20 minutes

INGREDIENTS:
3 oz/75 g low-fat cream cheese
4 oz/125 g prawns
black pepper
8 oz/225 g dates, stones removed

METHOD
1   Place the cheese, prawns and pepper in a blender and process until smooth.
2   Pipe the mixture into the dates using a fluted nozzle and place in the refrigerator until required.

Stuffed Prunes

(makes 30 approximately)

PREPARATION TIME: 20 minutes

INGREDIENTS:
6 oz/175 g low-fat cream cheese
2 oz/50 g Gouda cheese, grated
2 oz/50 g walnuts, chopped
black pepper
8 oz/225 g ready-to-eat prunes, stones removed

METHOD
1   Place the cheeses, walnuts and pepper in a blender and process until smooth.
2   Pipe the mixture into the prunes using a fluted nozzle and place in the refrigerator until required.

Filo Rolls

(F 80)

PREPARATION TIME: 1½ hours
COOKING TIME: 15 minutes
TEMPERATURE: 220°C/425°F/Gas 7

INGREDIENTS:
1 lb/450 g fresh spinach, blanched, drained and finely chopped
6 oz/175 g Ricotta cheese, crumbled
6 oz/175 g Edam cheese, grated
2 oz/50 g Feta cheese, crumbled
4 spring onions, finely chopped
1 tsp fresh parsley, chopped
black pepper and nutmeg to taste
8 oz/225 g filo pastry
2 oz/50 g low-fat cooking spread, melted

METHOD

1   Mix together all the ingredients except the pastry and cooking spread.

2   Carefully unfold the sheets of filo pastry and cut into 4 width-ways, giving strips measuring 8 in × 3 in/200 mm × 800 mm. Keep the filo strips not in use under a damp tea towel to prevent them from drying out.

3   Working with one strip of filo at a time, brush each with the melted cooking spread and place a teaspoon of the cheese mixture about 1 in/25 mm from one of the short edges. Turn the edge up to cover it and fold the sides of the filo towards the middle. Roll it up to make a small parcel.

4   Brush with melted cooking spread once again and place on a lightly greased baking sheet, seam side down.

5   Bake until crisp and golden brown.

Savoury Tartlets

(24)

PREPARATION TIME: 45 minutes
COOKING TIME: 15 minutes
TEMPERATURE: 220°C/425°F/Gas 7

INGREDIENTS:
1 qty low-fat pastry (see p. 101)
8 oz/225 g tin asparagus, drained and chopped
6 oz/175 g crab meat
black pepper
1 tbsp low-calorie mayonnaise
24 small sprigs fresh dill

METHOD

1   Roll out the pastry and cut into 24 circles using a 2 in/50 mm fluted cutter. Lightly oil some tartlet tins and line with the pastry. Prick each with a fork and bake blind for 15 minutes. Cool on a wire tray.

2 Mix together the asparagus and crab meat. Season to taste with the black pepper.
3 Spread a little of the mayonnaise in the base of each pastry case and divide the crab mixture between the cases. Garnish with a sprig of dill.

Savoury Boats

(24)

PREPARATION TIME: 45 minutes
COOKING TIME: 15 minutes
TEMPERATURE: 220°C/425°F/Gas 7

INGREDIENTS:
1 qty low-fat pastry (see p. 101)
6 oz/175 g prawns, finely chopped
1 tbsp fresh tarragon, chopped
1 tbsp Greek strained yogurt
black pepper
24 sprigs fresh tarragon

METHOD
1 Lightly oil 24 boat-shaped tartlet tins.
2 Roll out the pastry and use to line the tartlet tins. Prick each with a fork and bake blind. Cool on a wire tray.
3 Mix together the prawns, tarragon, yogurt and black pepper. Spoon into the pastry boats and garnish with the tarragon sprigs.

Mangetout with Smoked Salmon

(makes about 100)

PREPARATION TIME: 1 hour
CHILLING TIME: 2 hours

INGREDIENTS:
12 oz/350 g mangetout, washed and topped and tailed
3 oz/75 g smoked salmon offcuts
8 oz/225 g fromage frais
1 tsp lemon zest
black pepper

METHOD

1   Steam the mangetout for 30 seconds only and place under cold running water for a minute to fix the colour. Drain and pat dry with kitchen roll. Keep in the refrigerator until required.
2   Place the salmon, fromage frais, lemon zest and pepper in a blender and process until smooth. Keep in the refrigerator for 2 hours.
3   Split each of the mangetout open along its edge, keeping one side intact. Pipe the salmon mixture into each pod with a fluted nozzle. Keep chilled until you are ready to serve.

A Selection of Canapés

Canapés, or mini open sandwiches, are invaluable little fillers at a drinks party. They look colourful and appetizing and are simple to prepare. Canapés consist of three distinct layers: the base, a spread which binds the base to the final layer, the topping. The variations are endless. Canapé bases can be made of pastry, cheese, biscuit, bread and vegetables, while the toppings could be cheese-, fruit-, fish-, meat- and vegetable-based. Here are just a few ideas for you to experiment with.

BASES
cheese pastry
herb pastry
wholemeal pastry
toasted wholemeal bread
pumpernickel
mini melba toasts
mini pitta breads
crisprolls
rye bread
crispbread
cucumber slices
celery pieces
carrot slices
courgette slices
Edam cheese
Gouda cheese
low-fat cheese slices
oatmeal biscuits
cheese biscuits

Canapé bases should ideally be ¼ in/5mm thick and 1½ in/40 mm in diameter. Many different shapes can be made: squares, rectangles, triangles, circles, diamonds, hearts – anything you like, even tiny teddy bear shapes!

SPREADS
Mix together 4 oz/100 g of low-fat soft cheese with any of the following:

1 tbsp watercress, chopped
1 spring onion, chopped
•
2 oz/50 g tuna fish, mashed
1 tbsp low-calorie mayonnaise
black pepper
•
2 oz/50 g smoked mackerel, mashed
1 lemon, zest of

2 garlic cloves, crushed
black pepper

•

2 oz/50 g prawns, finely chopped
1 tsp anchovy paste

•

2 oz/50 g apple, grated

Mix together 4 oz/100 g of low-fat spread with any of the following:

2 oz/50 g walnuts, finely chopped
1 orange, zest of

•

2 tsp garam masala

•

2 oz/50 g spinach, blanched and finely chopped
½ tsp nutmeg

•

2 oz/50 g smoked salmon offcuts, chopped
2 tsp lemon juice
black pepper

•

2 garlic cloves, crushed
1 tbsp chives, chopped

Spreads should be made at least 3 hours in advance to allow the flavours to blend and should be stored in a refrigerator. The basic 4 oz/100 g of soft cheese or low-fat spread will be enough for approximately 25 canapé bases.

TOPPINGS
6 oz/175 g prawns
Place 2 prawns on each canapé.

•

6 oz/175 g crab, flaked
1 tbsp low-calorie mayonnaise
1 lemon, zest of

Combine all the ingredients and place a teaspoon of the mixture on each canapé.

6 oz/175 g sardines, drained and mashed
1 orange, zest of

Mix together well and place a teaspoonful on each canapé.

•

4 oz/100 g smoked salmon

Cut into strips and roll up. Place a salmon roll on each canapé.

•

1 red apple, sliced finely
1 tbsp lemon juice
4 oz/100 g smoked mackerel, flaked
1 tbsp fromage frais

Top each canapé with a small apple slice brushed with lemon juice, a few flakes of smoked mackerel and a little fromage frais.

•

3 oz/75 g chicken, cooked and minced
1 oz/25 g apple, grated
1 oz/25 g almonds, chopped
2 tbsp fromage frais

Mix all the ingredients together and place a little on each canapé.

•

4 oz/100 g smoked chicken, cooked and minced
1 tbsp low-calorie mayonnaise

Mix together the ingredients and top each canapé with a teaspoonful.

•

4 oz/100 g smoked chicken, cooked and minced
1 tsp curry paste
1 tbsp fromage frais
1 oz/25 g raisins

Mix the ingredients together and place a little on each canapé.

•

4 oz/100 g turkey, cooked and cut into small slices
25 mandarin orange segments

Place a small slice of turkey on each canapé and top with a mandarin segment.

4 oz/100 g Edam cheese, grated
1 red apple, grated
1 tbsp lemon juice
1 tsp garam masala
25 walnut halves

Mix together the first 4 ingredients and place a little on each
canapé. Top with a walnut half.

•

4 oz/100 g asparagus pieces
2 tbsp fromage frais
black pepper to taste

Mix the ingredients together and place a little on each canapé.

•

4 oz/100 g cottage cheese
3 oz/75 g fresh mango, finely chopped

Mix the cottage cheese with the mango and top each canapé with a
spoonful of the mixture.

•

4 oz/100 g cottage cheese
2 oz/50 g toasted sunflower seeds
10 black olives, stoned and chopped

Mix all the ingredients together and pile on to each canapé.

A whole variety of vegetables and fruits can be used as toppings.
Why not try radish, watercress, peppers, tomato, kiwi fruit,
lychee, passion fruit, peaches, apricots, cherries and prunes? In
fact, use anything that takes your fancy, and garnish with fresh
herbs and zests of fruits. The quantities given in the recipes will
make enough for approximately 25 canapés.

Melon and Cheese Squares

(32)

PREPARATION TIME: 30 minutes

INGREDIENTS:
8 slices low-fat processed cheese
1 tsp ground ginger
32 1 in/25 mm cubes of melon
32 cocktail sticks

METHOD
1   Cut the slices of cheese into 4, making 32 strips in all.
2   Sprinkle a little ground ginger on each melon cube and wrap a cheese slice around it. Secure with a cocktail stick.

Stuffed Cherry Tomatoes

(makes 30)

PREPARATION TIME: 60 minutes

INGREDIENTS:
30 cherry tomatoes, washed and dried
6 oz/175 g tuna in brine, drained
1 tbsp low-calorie mayonnaise
black pepper
1 tbsp fresh basil, chopped
4 tsp lemon zest

METHOD
1   Cut a thin slice off the base of each tomato and remove the seeds.
2   Place the tuna, mayonnaise, black pepper, basil and 1 teaspoon of the lemon zest in a blender and process until smooth.
3   Spoon, or pipe, the tuna mixture into the hollowed-out

tomatoes and garnish with the remaining lemon zest. Keep in the refrigerator until required.

CHEESE CHART

Cheese	Serving (g)	Calories	Fat (g)
14% fat cheese (Cheddar type)	100	250	14.0
11% fat cheese (Edam type)	100	245	11.0
9% fat singles	100	195	9.0
Bavarian blue cheese	100	215	12.5
Bavarian whipped soft cheese	100	310	30.0
Brie	100	300	25.0
Brie extra creamy	100	419	39.5
Cheddar:			
English slices	100	405	33.0
Farmhouse	100	410	34.0
English mature	100	405	34.1
Irish medium	100	405	33.1
Medium-matured coloured English	100	405	33.1
Medium-matured English	100	410	34.0
Mild English	100	405	34.4
Cheese spread with walnuts	100	310	26.5
Cheese spread	per portion	45	3.5
Cheese spread	100	290	25.0
Cheshire:			
coloured and white	100	380	31.0
Cottage cheese:	100	100	4.0
and prawns	100	150	10.1
with chives	100	95	4.1
with cucumber/celery/onion	100	85	3.4
with pineapple	100	95	3.6
with salmon/cucumber	100	110	5.9
with onions and peppers	100	85	3.6
Cottage cheese, half fat:	100	85	1.5
and pineapple	100	85	1.3
and vegetable	100	75	1.3

Cheese	Serving (g)	Calories	Fat (g)
Cracker snack	100	410	35.3
Cream cheese:	100	435	45.0
with chives	100	435	45.0
with pineapple	100	380	38.0
Creamery:	100	310	30.0
with herbs and garlic	100	310	30.0
Half fat	100	180	15.0
Curd cheese	100	170	12.0
Danish blue	100	355	29.5
Danish mycella	100	380	34.1
Dolcelatte	100	355	27.0
Double Gloucester	100	375	31.8
Doux de montagne	100	375	28.0
Edam	100	330	24.0
Full-fat soft cheese	100	305	29.5
Gorgonzola	100	345	29.0
Gouda	100	350	28.0
Havarti	100	415	37.0
Jutland blue	100	380	35.0
Leicester with walnuts	100	380	32.3
Mozzarella	100	275	19.0
Pipo creme	100	320	25.5
Port Salut	100	330	25.9
Processed cheese slices	100	320	24.0
Roquefort	100	380	32.0
Skimmed milk soft cheese	100	80	0.5
Somerset goat's cheese, natural	100	310	25.0
Stilton	100	375	31.8
St Paulin	100	295	21.0
Svenbo	100	380	29.1
Welsh goat's cheese	100	305	22.8

Information courtesy of Sainsbury plc.

CHAPTER TEN

The Festive Season

Christmas has always been my favourite time of year. It holds for me a certain magic, almost a mysticism, filled with ancient traditions, fables and fantasies that everyone, whatever age, can escape into. It's simply wonderful. And when there is a crisp blanket of snow glistening in the winter sunshine it makes Christmas seem even more special.

Our home is decked out with boughs of holly and anything else that I can lay my hands on. I think it's fair to say that I do go over the top – but then it's such good fun, isn't it? The Christmas tree is the focal point and so it has to be the best there is. I will wander the streets of all the local towns and villages searching for that certain one that has the right shape, colour and character. And then it's down to the decorations. The very mention of tree decorations is a sore point in our house. A few years ago we were on holiday in Singapore – a bargain hunter's paradise. My fellow travellers were frantically buying designer clothes and jewellery, having silk suits made and electronic gadgets shipped home to England. But there is always one exception and I was it. You see, I had found this amazing store called Tangs with the most elaborate Santa's Grotto you can imagine: my eyes stood out like the proverbial chapel hat pegs. I spent two of our three days in Singapore in that grotto. And, of course, instead of the designer gear to carry home I had two suitcases jam-packed full of Christmas decorations the like of which you cannot imagine. They are simply beautiful. Unfortunately, I was stopped at Customs (Murphy's Law, I think it's called), and was treated particularly suspiciously. After all, who on earth would go all the way to the Far East only to bring back Christmas decorations? They thought that my tree lights and silk baubles were concealing drugs. You should have seen the expression on the faces of the Customs men; what a picture – if only I'd bought a camera! I don't know why but such things always seem to be happening to me; no wonder one of my nicknames is 'Bungle'.

BACK TO BASICS

Christmas, above all else, is a time for the family to congregate and enjoy themselves. Unfortunately, though, it is also an extremely busy time and so planning is crucial. I think that our family is quite normal in that we eat far too much, drink too much and sit watching television – usually *The Wizard of Oz* for the fiftieth time. And we all get really fed up with turkey for breakfast, lunch, dinner and sandwiches for the next two months, not to mention the turkey soup! With this in mind, I have planned a 'one-off' chicken dish for the festival meal on Christmas Day. The spirit and tradition of the dinner are retained while avoiding all the left-overs. A bonus is that it carves up quickly and easily.

Why not ring the changes on Christmas Eve by making an Oriental meal? It really does make a nice change, and a bonus is that it is both quick and easy to prepare. Instead of left-overs for the Boxing Day Dinner I have invented a refreshing crab mousse for the starter, followed by chicken balls in a fruity orange sauce. The orange theme of the main course really does cleanse the palate after the Christmas eating binge. And with fruit pancakes as the dessert you really are on to a winner!

I for one do not believe in running myself ragged at Christmas, after all, I want to enjoy it as well. The master plan is to prepare whatever I can in advance, and store or freeze it. It not only cuts down on the work itself on the big day, but also reduces panic attacks! Sauces are no problem at all because I make them weeks before and simply freeze them. The Christmas pud and cake store well anyway, and so can be made in November. The mince pies, stuffed boned chicken and festive loaf can be made weeks ahead and frozen. On the day all you have to do is set the table, cook the vegetables, reheat or defrost the remaining food and organize the drinks. Then comes the aftermath – all that washing-up. Never mind, many hands make light work.

Christmas deserves the best of everything. So out with your best china, best glassware and cutlery, most elegant tablecloth and napkins. To finish the setting you must have an eye-catching table decoration. I tend not to use fresh flowers at Christmastime because they are so expensive. Use dried flowers and candles with holly thrown in for good measure. And of course, don't forget the mistletoe. Merry Christmas!

CHRISTMAS EVE DINNER
FOR SIX

Menu

FISH BALL SOUP

PEPPERED CHICKEN
WITH
COUNTRY RICE

ORIENTAL FRUITS WITH TOFU

COFFEE OR TEA

Fish Ball Soup
(F 8)

PREPARATION TIME: 15 minutes
COOKING TIME: 10 minutes

INGREDIENTS:
12 oz/350 g monkfish, cut into cubes
1 tbsp dry sherry
1 tbsp fresh ginger, grated
½ onion, minced
4 fl oz/125 ml cold water
½ tsp low-sodium salt
1 egg white
2 tsp sunflower oil
1¼ tbsp cornflour
2pt/1.2 l fish stock
6 spring onions, shredded
4 oz/125 g peeled prawns

METHOD
1   Place the fish in a food processor with the dry sherry.
2   Pop the ginger and minced onion into a piece of muslin and squeeze over the fish until the juice is extracted. Add the water and salt and blend until smooth.
3   Add the egg white, oil and cornflour and blend again.
4   Form the mixture into walnut-sized balls.
5   Bring a large saucepan of water to the boil and drop in the fish balls. Simmer until they float to the surface and cook for a further 3 minutes. Lift them out of the pan with a slotted spoon and discard the water.
6   Pour the fish stock into the pan and bring to the boil.
7   Add the shredded spring onion and the prawns to the pan with the fish balls and simmer for 5 minutes before serving.

Peppered Chicken

(F 6)

PREPARATION TIME: 10 minutes
MARINATING TIME: 2 hours
COOKING TIME: 25 minutes

INGREDIENTS:
6 chicken breasts, skinned
2 garlic cloves, crushed
2 tsp fresh ginger, minced
2 tsp black pepper
2 tbsp coriander, finely chopped
2 tsp sugar
2 tbsp dark soy sauce
1 tbsp sunflower oil

METHOD
1 Prick the chicken breasts with a skewer repeatedly to allow the seasonings to penetrate.
2 Mix together the garlic, ginger, pepper and coriander. Spread this mixture over the chicken breasts, place them in a dish and cover with clingfilm. Leave to stand for 2 hours.
3 Dissolve the sugar in the soy sauce and add the oil.
4 Remove the clingfilm from the chicken and brush with the oil mixture.
5 Cook the chicken under a hot grill, turning frequently and brushing with the oil mixture until the chicken is cooked and crispy on the surface.

Country Rice

(6)

PREPARATION TIME: 10 minutes
COOKING TIME: 20 minutes

INGREDIENTS:
12 oz/350 g brown rice
4 oz/125 g wild rice
3 tbsp olive oil
2 cinnamon sticks
3 whole cloves
½ tsp cardamom seeds
2 onions, peeled and sliced finely
4 garlic cloves, sliced
4 slices young fresh ginger
¾ tsp turmeric
1 tsp low-sodium salt
1 tsp black pepper
26 fl oz/750 ml chicken stock

METHOD
1 Wash the rice thoroughly and drain well.
2 Heat the oil in a large saucepan. Add the spices and fry for
   1 minute before stirring in the onion, garlic, ginger, turmeric,
   salt and pepper. Cook for a further 1 minute.
3 Add the rice and stir until each grain is coated with the oil.
   Pour in the stock and bring to the boil.
4 Cover and simmer until the liquid has been absorbed and the
   rice is cooked.
5 Give the rice a quick stir with a fork and serve.

Oriental Fruits with Tofu

(6)

PREPARATION TIME: 5 minutes

INGREDIENTS:
12 lychees, peeled and stones removed
1 kiwi fruit, peeled and sliced
1 mango, peeled and sliced
4 oz/125 g tofu, cubed
3 tsp rosewater

METHOD
Divide the fruits and tofu between 6 dessert dishes and sprinkle on the rosewater.

CHRISTMAS DAY DINNER FOR EIGHT

Menu

FESTIVE LOAF

STUFFED BONED CHICKEN
WITH
CREAMED BRUSSELS SPROUTS
CARROTS WITH LEMON
SAUTÉED POTATOES

CHRISTMAS PUDDING
WITH
RUM SAUCE

COFFEE OR TEA
WITH
LIQUEURS

CHRISTMAS CAKE
MINCE PIES

Festive Loaf
(F 8)

PREPARATION TIME: 1½ hours
COOKING TIME: 1½ hours
TEMPERATURE: 180°C/350°F/Gas 4

INGREDIENTS:

MUSHROOM AND SAGE LAYER:
2 tbsp extra virgin olive oil
1 bunch spring onions, washed and chopped
6 oz/175 g mushrooms, wiped and sliced
2 oz/50 g wholemeal breadcrumbs
2 tsp sage, chopped
1 tbsp sunflower seeds, toasted
1 tbsp tahini
1 tbsp skimmed milk
black pepper, freshly ground
1 tsp nutmeg, freshly grated

CRANBERRY AND APRICOT LAYER:
1 tbsp extra virgin olive oil
1 onion, peeled and finely chopped
4 oz/100 g fresh cranberries, washed
2 oz/50 g wholemeal breadcrumbs
2 oz/50 g walnuts, ground
2 oz/50 g dried apricots, soaked and chopped
1 tbsp tahini
1 tbsp skimmed milk
black pepper and low-sodium salt

SPLIT PEA LAYER:
1 tbsp extra virgin olive oil
1 onion, peeled and chopped
6 oz/175 g yellow split peas, washed, soaked and cooked
1 egg white
black pepper and low-sodium salt

METHOD

1 Lightly oil a 2 lb/900 g load tin.
2 *Mushroom layer*: Heat the oil and fry the spring onions for about 1 minute. Add the mushrooms and fry for a further 2 minutes.
3 In a bowl, mix in all the remaining ingredients, add the spring onions and mushrooms and put to one side.
4 *Cranberry and apricot layer:* Heat the oil and fry the onion until soft – about 2 minutes.
5 In a bowl, mix in all the remaining ingredients, add the onions and put to one side.
6 *Split pea layer:* Heat the oil and fry the onion until soft and add to the split peas.
7 Beat the egg white and add to the mixture. Season to taste.
8 Place the mushroom mixture in the base of the tin, pressing it down firmly.
9 Then add the cranberry layer, pressing down firmly.
10 Add the split pea layer, pressing down firmly. Cover with greased foil and bake for 90 minutes. Allow to cool for at least 10 minutes in the tin before turning out. Serve with cranberry sauce.

Stuffed Boned Chicken
(F 8)

PREPARATION TIME: 1 hour
COOKING TIME: 2 hours
TEMPERATURE: 190°C/375°F/Gas 5

INGREDIENTS:
1 oz/25 g low-fat cooking spread
1 level tbsp cornflour
¼ pt/150 ml skimmed milk
4 oz/125 g chicken breast, finely minced
4 oz/125 g chestnut purée
2 egg whites
4 oz/125 g mushrooms, chopped finely
1 red pepper, seeded and chopped
1 oz/25 g walnuts, broken
black pepper and low-sodium salt
1 × 3½–4 lb/1.6–1.8 kg chicken, boned

METHOD
1 Melt the cooking spread in a saucepan and stir in the cornflour. Slowly add the milk, stirring continuously. Bring to the boil and simmer for a minute or two until thick. Remove from the heat and allow to cool for about 5 minutes.
2 Stir the sauce into the minced chicken and chestnut purée and beat in the egg whites. Fold in the mushrooms, red pepper and walnuts. Season to taste.
3 Fill the chicken with the stuffing and sew the bird up with string. Place in a roasting tin, with a couple of tablespoons of hot water in the bottom, and cook for about 2 hours. If the chicken looks too brown, simply cover with foil.
4 Serve either hot or cold, remembering to remove the string before carving.

Creamed Brussels Sprouts

(8)

PREPARATION TIME: 15 minutes
COOKING TIME: 55 minutes
TEMPERATURE: 180°C/350°F/Gas 4

INGREDIENTS:
2 lb/900 g Brussels sprouts
½ pt/275 ml skimmed milk
2 slices of onion
2 bay leaves
8 peppercorns
2 oz/50 g low-fat cooking spread
2 tbsp wholemeal flour
black pepper and low-sodium salt
½ tsp grated nutmeg
1 egg
1 egg white
1 oz/25 g wholemeal breadcrumbs

METHOD

1 Trim the sprouts and wash. Steam for 5 minutes until tender. Chop finely.
2 Meanwhile, bring the milk to the boil with the onion, bay leaves and peppercorns. Remove from the heat and leave to infuse for 10 minutes.
3 Melt 1 oz/25 g of the cooking spread and stir in the flour. Cook for 1 minute, stirring. Remove from the heat and gradually stir in the strained milk and seasoning.
4 Bring to the boil and cook until the sauce thickens. Remove from the heat and stir in the chopped sprouts with the nutmeg. Adjust the seasoning and beat in the eggs.
5 Spoon into a lightly oiled 3 pt/1.7 l soufflé dish and sprinkle with the breadcrumbs. Dot with the remaining cooking spread and bake for about 50 minutes.

Carrots with Lemon

(8)

PREPARATION TIME: 15 minutes
COOKING TIME: 15 minutes

INGREDIENTS:
2 oz/50 g low-fat cooking spread
1½ lb/700 g carrots, washed and cut into strips
1 lemon, juice and zest of
½ tsp grated nutmeg
4 fl oz/100 ml natural low-fat yogurt
black pepper and low-sodium salt
1 tbsp fresh parsley, chopped

METHOD

1　Melt the low-fat cooking spread in a saucepan and add the carrots. Cover and sauté gently for about 15 minutes. Shake the pan occasionally to avoid any sticking.

2　Stir in the lemon juice, zest, nutmeg and yogurt. Season to taste and heat through gently. Serve immediately sprinkled with the chopped parsley.

Sautéed Potatoes
(8)

PREPARATION TIME: 15 minutes
COOKING TIME: 20 minutes

INGREDIENTS:
3 lb/1.5 kg potatoes, medium size
4 tbsp olive oil
1 oz/25 g low-fat cooking spread
black pepper and low-sodium salt
4 tbsp fresh mint, chopped

METHOD
1   Scrub the potatoes and place in a large pan of cold salted water. Bring to the boil and cook for 20 minutes.
2   Drain and keep warm.
3   Cut into large wedge-shaped pieces. Heat the oil in a large frying pan, add the low-fat cooking spread and spoon in the potatoes.
4   Fry over a moderate heat, turning occasionally, until golden brown. Remove from the pan and blot off any surplus fat with kitchen roll. Season well and serve with the mint.

Christmas Pudding

(F 10)

PREPARATION TIME: 1 hour
COOKING TIME: 4 hours plus 3 hours before serving

INGREDIENTS:
8 oz/225 g dried dates
5 fl oz/150 ml rum
8 oz/225 g low-fat cooking spread
2 egg whites
1 tbsp black molasses
1 lemon, juice of
2 lemons, zest of
2 oranges, zest of
4 oz/100 g currants
4 oz/100 g sultanas
4 oz/125 g wholemeal breadcrumbs
4 oz/125 g wholemeal flour
½ tsp ground ginger
½ tsp grated nutmeg
1 tsp cinnamon
2 tsp mixed spice

METHOD

1 Place the dates in a small saucepan with the rum and heat gently for about 5 minutes until soft and pulpy. Leave to cool slightly.
2 Cream together the dates and cooking spread. Beat in the egg whites, molasses, lemon juice and fruit zest.
3 Add all the remaining ingredients and stir well.
4 Place the mixture into a well-greased 2 pt/900 ml pudding basin and cover with greased, greaseproof paper. Tie down well with string.
5 Steam for 4 hours.
6 Store the pudding in a cool dry place.
7 Steam again for another 3 hours prior to serving. Serve hot with rum sauce.

Rum Sauce

(makes 1 pt/550 ml)

PREPARATION TIME: 5 minutes
COOKING TIME: 5 minutes

INGREDIENTS:
4 tbsp cornflour
½ pt/275 ml skimmed milk
½ pt/275 ml soya milk
1½ tbsp sugar
4 tbsp rum

METHOD
1   Place the cornflour in a basin and blend with 2 tbsp of milk to a smooth paste.
2   Heat the remaining skimmed and soya milk until boiling. Pour on to the blended cornflour, stirring continuously.
3   Return the mixture to the pan and bring to the boil, stirring all the time. Cook for about 2 minutes after the mixture has thickened. Add the sugar and stir in the rum.

Christmas Cake

PREPARATION TIME: 30 minutes
COOKING TIME: 1½ hours
TEMPERATURE: 160°C/325°F/Gas 3

INGREDIENTS:
8 oz/225 g dried dates
½ pt/275 ml water
4 oz/100 g raisins
2 oz/50 g dried apricots, finely chopped
4 oz/100 g grated carrot
2 oz/50 g stem ginger, finely chopped
4 oz/100 g walnuts, broken
6 oz/175 g plain wholemeal flour
4 tsp low-sodium baking powder
2 tsp ground cinnamon
1 tsp mixed spice
1 orange, zest of
1 lemon, zest of
4 tbsp brandy

METHOD

1   Lightly grease a 2 lb/900 g loaf tin (or round cake tin) and line with greased, greaseproof paper.

2   Place the dates in a small saucepan with the water and bring to the boil. Simmer until they are soft and pulpy – about 7 minutes. Leave to cool slightly.

3   Put the dates, dried fruits, carrot, ginger, walnuts, flour, baking powder, cinnamon, spice, zest and brandy into a bowl and mix well.

4   Spoon into the prepared tin, level top and bake for about 1½ hours. The cake is cooked when a skewer inserted into its centre is clean when removed. Cool on a wire tray.

5   You could decorate the cake in the usual way with marzipan and icing. I prefer to be a little different. Try brushing a little warmed sugar-free apricot jam on to the top of the cake and arrange nuts, glacé fruits and dried fruits on the top. Brush with a little warm honey to glaze and finish with a red ribbon around the edge tied in a bow.

Mince Pies

(F 40)

PREPARATION TIME: 30 minutes
COOKING TIME: 30 minutes
TEMPERATURE: 200°C/400°F/Gas 6

INGREDIENTS:
8 oz/225 g currants
8 oz/225 g sultanas
1 lb/450 g grated apple
3 tbsp fruit zest
2 oz/50 g dried dates, chopped
8 oz/225 g grated carrot
4 tbsp brandy
1 tsp grated nutmeg
½ tsp cinnamon
1 tsp ground ginger
2 oz/50 g flaked almonds
1 packet filo pastry (about 20 sheets)
1 tbsp safflower or sunflower oil

METHOD
1 Mix together all the ingredients except the pastry and oil and leave, covered, overnight.
2 Cut the filo sheets in half widthways and place under a damp cloth while not in use.
3 Lightly oil each filo sheet as you use it. Fold the filo sheet in half widthways and place a tablespoon of the mincemeat mixture in the centre. Gather each corner and edge of the filo and draw over the mincemeat. Nip together at the top and twist gently to form a 'cashbag' shape. Brush lightly with oil.
4 Repeat with the remaining filo squares.
5 Place on a lightly greased baking sheet and cook for about 20 minutes until golden. Serve warm.

BOXING DAY DINNER
FOR SIX

Menu

CRAB RING

CHICKEN BALLS IN ORANGE SAUCE
WITH
MANGETOUT WITH ORANGE
CREAMED POTATOES
BABY SWEETCORN WITH RED PEPPER

STUFFED BANANA PANCAKES

COFFEE OR TEA

Crab Ring

(6)

PREPARATION TIME: 25 minutes
COOKING TIME: 5 minutes
CHILLING TIME: 3 hours

INGREDIENTS:
½ pt/275 ml fish stock
4 spring onions, finely chopped
2 garlic cloves, crushed
1 tsp fresh dill, chopped
7 oz/200 g crab meat, mashed with a fork
gelatine
4 tbsp fromage frais
black pepper

METHOD

1 Warm the fish stock with the spring onions, garlic, dill and crab meat, stirring well.
2 Pour about 2 tablespoons of boiling water into a cup and sprinkle on the gelatine. Stir vigorously and leave to dissolve. Add to the crab mixture.
3 Place the crab mixture into a food processor and blend for a few seconds until fairly smooth.
4 Stir in the fromage frais and season with black pepper.
5 Pour the mixture into a 1 pt/550 ml ring mould or other suitable container and leave to set in the refrigerator. Turn out and serve.

Chicken Balls in Orange Sauce
(F 6)

PREPARATION TIME: 15 minutes
CHILLING TIME: 30 minutes
COOKING TIME: 40 minutes

INGREDIENTS:
1 lb/450 g chicken, finely minced
1 onion, finely chopped
4 oz/125 g wholemeal breadcrumbs
1 tbsp fresh tarragon, chopped
1 tbsp fresh chives, chopped
3 garlic cloves, crushed
low-sodium salt and black pepper
2 egg whites
2 tbsp low-fat natural yogurt
2 tbsp olive oil
1 red pepper, cut into thin strips
½ pt/275 ml chicken stock
¼ pt/150 ml fresh orange juice
½ orange, zest of
2 tsp cornflour

METHOD
1   Mix together the chicken, onion, breadcrumbs, herbs, garlic, seasoning, egg whites and yogurt. Form into balls, about the size of golf balls, and place in the refrigerator to chill.
2   Heat the olive oil in a saucepan. Add the chicken balls and cook until evenly browned. Add the strips of pepper and cook for a further minute.
3   Stir in the stock, orange juice and zest. Blend the cornflour with 2 teaspoons water and stir into the mixture.
4   Simmer for about 25 minutes until the chicken balls are cooked.

Mangetout with Orange

(6)

PREPARATION TIME: 5 minutes
COOKING TIME: 2 minutes

INGREDIENTS:
1 lb/450 g mangetout, topped and tailed
1 fresh orange, segments and zest

METHOD
Wash the mangetout and with the orange segments and zest steam over a pan of boiling water for two minutes.

Creamed Potatoes

(6)

PREPARATION TIME: 3 minutes
COOKING TIME: 25 minutes

INGREDIENTS:
1½ lb/700 g potatoes, washed
2 oz/50 g low-fat spread
black pepper
low-sodium salt
skimmed milk
1 tbsp fresh parsley, chopped

METHOD
1 Boil the potatoes in salted water until tender. Strain off the water.
2 Add the low-fat spread and seasoning before mashing well. Add enough skimmed milk to make a soft mixture.
3 Stir in the parsley and serve.

Baby Sweetcorn with Red Pepper
(F 6)

PREPARATION TIME: 2 minutes
COOKING TIME: 4 minutes

INGREDIENTS:
1 lb/500 g baby sweetcorn
1 red pepper

METHOD
1 Wash the vegetables.
2 Seed the red pepper and cut into strips.
3 Place the baby sweetcorn and red pepper in a steamer and steam over a pan of boiling water for about 4 minutes.

Stuffed Banana Pancakes

(6 – makes 12)

PREPARATION TIME: 20 minutes
STANDING TIME: 45 minutes
COOKING TIME: 25 minutes

INGREDIENTS:
2½ oz/65 g plain wholemeal flour
2½ oz/65 g plain white flour
2 eggs
½ pt/275 ml skimmed milk
1 tsp sunflower oil
2 bananas, chopped
½ lemon, juice of
6 tbsp Greek strained yogurt
6 tsp olive oil

METHOD
1 Place the flours, eggs, milk and sunflower oil in a food processor and blend until smooth. Leave to stand for 45 minutes.
2 Meanwhile coat the chopped bananas with the lemon juice and mix with the yogurt. Place in the refrigerator until required.
3 Using the olive oil lightly oil a 7 in/18 cm frying pan and pour in enough batter to cover the base thinly. Cook each side of the pancake for about 1 minute over a high heat.
4 When each pancake is cooked blot off any excess oil with a sheet of kitchen roll before placing on a plate and popping into the oven at a low temperature to keep warm until all are made.
5 Place a spoonful of the yogurt mixture on to one half of each pancake and fold over. Serve immediately.

This recipe works equally well with any fresh fruit, either singly or in combination.

CHAPTER ELEVEN

The Great Escape

THE BEST OF BARBECUES

A barbecue conjures up images of lovely summer days with bright red poppies swaying gently in the breeze. The fish and burgers are sizzling on the barbecue and the smell – oh, that unmistakable smell of burning charcoal and wood mingling with the culinary delights. Sounds just too good to be true, doesn't it? And with our English summers it probably is. The reality is usually something quite different.

Barbecues are wonderful, the height of informality where people mingle happily and chat about everything and nothing. And, for me, there isn't anything to compare to eating outdoors in the fresh air.

I attended a local village barbecue recently and had an absolutely marvellous time. Everyone was clad in jeans, warm jumpers and anoraks – it was the middle of June! We did brave the elements for a while and then the weather took a slight turn for the worse. We promptly moved indoors to the village hall. The community spirit took over and everyone rallied around organizing the event. Makeshift wooden tables and chairs were hastily arranged and candles provided the lighting. It really did look lovely – and very romantic.

At frequent intervals a rhythmic thudding sound echoed through the hall and I for one was intrigued by it. One thing was for sure, you certainly couldn't dance to it! Upon investigation I traced this strange sound to a poor old chap who was looking after the drinks table. Every time someone ordered a pint of beer his face developed a frown – and I'm not surprised. You see, there was a foot pump under the table and this poor old chap had to go 'hell for leather' to draw a drink. After a couple of pints his leg must have really ached. It explained his slightly odd walk anyway!

The food was excellent. Yes, there were the obligatory beef-burgers, sausages and shish kebabs but there were also lots of lovely salads, baked potatoes, crispy French bread and chicken to enjoy. It was hilarious watching people trying to eat their food, which was precariously balanced on paper plates, with plastic knives and forks that kept on snapping. People were embarrassed and perplexed as they pondered how to eat the meal. It didn't take too long before everyone resorted to fingers – the only way to eat barbecued food in my opinion. That's entertainment at its very best.

The moral of this cautionary tale is not to wait for that perfect English summer's day, but to get on with it regardless. Make sure that you have an indoor venue nearby just in case.

BACK TO BASICS

Barbecues are fun, exciting and easy but you do need to consider one or two things. For instance, where are you going to site it? A word of warning: don't have it near anything flammable, including trees, or you could finish up with a bigger barbecue than you anticipated. Keep to open spaces which are also sheltered from the wind. Now I know that I should be encouraging exercise but, to save your legs and time, it is better to site the barbecue near to the kitchen area. And, just in case weather forecasters get it wrong, try and put it near to an alternative venue with a roof!

It's a good idea to have some kind of seating available even if it's only a case of makeshift tables, using old doors (remember to take the knobs off though), and milk crates for chairs. It all adds to the atmosphere, doesn't it? Something else which adds atmosphere is candles. Candles in jam jars, on window ledges and tables – anywhere in fact. You can also buy flares which stick into the ground and last for hours – they look great. It's a nice way of lighting an evening barbecue, and is much softer than electric lighting.

Something to remember about the quantities of food is that the fresh air will really heighten people's appetites. A good guide is to think of what you would prepare for an indoor get-together and then double it. Paper plates are a bit of a disaster at barbecues as the hot food tends to make them disintegrate. Laminated paper plates or china ones are much better for the job. In my book, fingers beat plastic knives and forks any day of the week, but do provide plenty of paper napkins. Otherwise use regular cutlery please.

The barbecue should be up to temperature about twenty minutes after the guests arrive. Different models vary but allow about forty minutes for the coals to form the uniform grey ash signifying the correct temperature has been reached. Gas barbecues take only about twenty minutes. It's all a matter of trial and error and you soon get the hang of it. The one thing that always seems to happen at a barbecue is that the men take over the cooking completely – and that's certainly fine by me!

THE BARBECUE

Menu

MONKFISH KEBABS
PRAWN AND CHICKEN KEBABS
MACKEREL WITH ORANGE AND FENNEL
FISH CAKES
MARINATED CHICKEN
CHICKEN BURGERS
HERBED TURKEY ESCALOPES
VEGETABLE KEBABS
BARBECUED VEGETABLES
SPICED POTATO SALAD
EMERALD SALAD
FRUITY SALAD

HERBY TOMATO SAUCE
SWEET AND SOUR SAUCE
CHILLI SAUCE

BARBECUED APPLES
HOT BANANAS
FRUIT KEBABS

Monkfish Kebabs

(6)

PREPARATION TIME: 35 minutes
MARINATING TIME: 3 hours
COOKING TIME: 10 minutes

INGREDIENTS:
1 lb/450 g monkfish
12 sardines
12 cooked, unshelled prawns
12 courgette chunks, about 1 in/25 mm thick
12 bay leaves

MARINADE:
¼ pt/150 ml sesame seed oil
5 tbsp lemon juice
2 lemons, zest of
freshly ground black pepper
1 tbsp fresh dill, chopped
1 tbsp fresh rosemary
6 juniper berries, crushed

METHOD
1 Cut the monkfish into 1 in/25 mm cubes and place in a bowl with the sardines, prawns and courgettes.
2 Make the marinade by mixing together the oil, lemon juice, lemon zest, pepper, herbs and juniper berries.
3 Pour the marinade over the fish, cover and leave in a cool place for about 3 hours.
4 Drain the fish just prior to cooking.
5 Divide the monkfish between 6 long skewers and using 2 sardines, 2 courgette chunks, 2 prawns and 2 bay leaves for each kebab, thread the ingredients alternately on to the skewers.
6 Cook the kebabs over a moderately hot barbecue for about 10 minutes, turning once during cooking.
7 Serve hot on a plate of boiled wild rice, garnished with lemon wings and cucumber pieces.

Prawn and Chicken Kebabs

(6)

PREPARATION TIME: 20 minutes
MARINATING TIME: 2 hours
COOKING TIME: 15 minutes

INGREDIENTS:
1¾ lb/800 g chicken, cut into 1 in/25 mm cubes
18 cooked, unshelled prawns

MARINADE:
2 tbsp olive oil
2 garlic cloves, crushed
2 tbsp lemon juice
1 tbsp lemon zest
black pepper

METHOD
1   Place the cubed chicken in a bowl.
2   Mix together the marinade ingredients and pour the mixture over the chicken. Leave in a cool place for about 1½ hours, covered.
3   After 1½ hours add the prawns to the chicken in the marinade and leave for another ½ hour.
4   Thread chicken cubes and prawns on to 6 long skewers. Leave on a moderately hot barbecue for about 15 minutes, until the chicken is cooked. Turn once during cooking. Serve hot.

Mackerel with Orange and Fennel
(F 6)

PREPARATION TIME: 25 minutes
MARINATING TIME: 2 hours
COOKING TIME: 15 minutes

INGREDIENTS:
6 mackerel, cleaned but with heads remaining
4 tbsp olive oil
1 tbsp orange zest
black pepper
3 tbsp freshly chopped fennel
6 sprays fresh fennel

METHOD

1 Make diagonal slashes on each side of the fish – cutting right into the flesh – and lay in a shallow dish.
2 Mix together the oil, orange zest, pepper and chopped fennel and pour over the fish. Cover and leave in a cool place for about 2 hours to marinate. Turn once during marination.
3 Just prior to cooking, remove the fish from the marinade and place a piece of fresh fennel inside each fish and press a small sprig into the slashes.
4 Cook on a moderately hot barbecue for about 8 minutes on each side until the fish are cooked through. Take care when turning the fish as they can easily break up. Serve hot with crusty garlic bread and salads.

Fish Cakes
(F 12)

PREPARATION TIME: 40 minutes
CHILLING TIME: 45 minutes or overnight
COOKING TIME: 15 minutes

INGREDIENTS:
1 lb/450 g smoked mackerel
6 spring onions, finely chopped
6 tbsp firm mashed potato
2 lemons, zest of
1 tbsp fresh dill, chopped
black pepper and low-sodium salt

COATING:
1 egg, beaten
4 tbsp wholemeal breadcrumbs
1 tbsp sesame seeds

METHOD

1 Flake the smoked mackerel, being careful to remove all the bones.
2 Mix with the onions, potato, lemon zest, dill and seasonings.
3 Mix the breadcrumbs and sesame seeds together. With floured hands shape the fish mixture into 12 cakes and brush each with the beaten egg before coating with the breadcrumbs.
4 Leave to chill in the refrigerator for at least 45 minutes or, even better, overnight.
5 Cook the fish cakes on a moderately hot barbecue for about 15 minutes, turning once. Be careful when turning them over as they are quite fragile.

Marinated Chicken

(F 6)

PREPARATION TIME: 20 minutes
MARINATING TIME: 3 hours or overnight
COOKING TIME: 15 minutes

INGREDIENTS:
6 chicken breasts, skinned and cut into 2 in/5 cm slices
3 tbsp sesame seed oil

MARINADE:
2 tbsp tamari
4 tbsp medium sherry
6 tbsp dry white wine
3 garlic cloves, crushed
10 spring onions, finely chopped
1 tsp dried rosemary
4 juniper berries, crushed (optional)

METHOD

1   Mix all the marinade ingredients together well and place in a shallow dish.

2   Put the chicken slices into the marinade and leave covered in a cool place for at least 3 hours. Turn occasionally.

3   Just prior to cooking, remove the chicken from the marinade and thread the meat on to 6 long skewers. Brush lightly with oil.

4   Cook on a moderately hot barbecue for about 8 minutes on each side until the chicken is cooked through.

5   Use the marinade as a sauce: heat in a saucepan and simmer for about 5 minutes.

6   Serve the chicken off the skewers piled on to a bed of boiled brown rice, with the sauce served separately.

Chicken Burgers

(F 6)

PREPARATION TIME: 25 minutes
COOKING TIME: 20 minutes

INGREDIENTS:
1 egg, beaten
2 tsp freshly chopped tarragon
black pepper
1½ oz/40 g wholemeal breadcrumbs
2 lb/900 g chicken, minced finely

METHOD
1   Mix together the egg, tarragon and black pepper and stir into the breadcrumbs.
2   Add this egg mixture to the minced chicken and stir well.
3   Divide the mixture into 6 portions and shape into 'burgers'. Chill in the refrigerator until you are ready to cook them.
4   Cook on a moderately hot barbecue for 8 minutes on each side, until they are cooked through.
5   Serve hot either in wholemeal baps or with garlic bread.

Herbed Turkey Escalopes
(F 6)

PREPARATION TIME: 20 minutes
COOKING TIME: 35 minutes

INGREDIENTS:
2 tbsp wholegrain mustard
4 tbsp natural low-fat yogurt
12 turkey escalopes
black pepper
2 tbsp fresh parsley, chopped
1 tbsp fresh tarragon, chopped
1 tbsp fresh rosemary, chopped
1 tbsp fresh basil, chopped
1 tbsp fresh chervil, chopped
1 lime, zest and juice of

METHOD

1   Mix together the mustard and yogurt. Coat the turkey escalopes with the mixture.
2   Place 2 pieces of the turkey in the centre of a large square of lightly oiled foil. Season well with pepper and sprinkle some chopped herbs over the top, followed by a little lime zest and juice. Prepare the remaining escalopes in the same way.
3   Wrap the foil tightly around the turkey and cook on a moderately hot barbecue for about 35 minutes, until tender.
4   Serve in the foil.

Vegetable Kebabs
(6)

SOAKING TIME: 30 minutes
PREPARATION TIME: 20 minutes
COOKING TIME: 10 minutes

INGREDIENTS:
2 tbsp olive oil or sesame seed oil
2 tsp mixed fresh herbs, chopped
18 baby corn on the cobs
18 courgette chunks approximately 2 in/50 mm thick
18 aubergine cubes approximately ½ in/10 mm thick
12 bay leaves
18 pieces of red pepper approximately 2 in/50 mm thick
12 dried prunes, pitted, soaked for 30 minutes

METHOD
1   Mix together the oil and herbs.
2   Divide the ingredients into 6 and carefully thread, alternately, on to 6 long skewers.
3   Brush the skewered vegetables with the oil mixture.
4   Cook over a moderately hot barbecue for about 10 minutes, turning once.
5   The kebabs are delicious served off the skewer inside warm pitta bread pockets.

Barbecued Vegetables

COURGETTES

Wash and top and tail the courgettes. Small courgettes can be either sliced in half lengthways or used whole, while large ones should be cut into thick slices. Brush lightly with herbed oil, impale them on skewers and cook over a hot barbecue for about 8 minutes, turning once.

PEPPERS

Wash the peppers and cut small ones in half, large ones into quarters. Remove the seeds. Brush lightly with herbed oil and thread on to skewers. Cook for about 3 minutes on a hot barbecue, turning once.

SWEETCORN

Baby sweetcorn can be used whole, brushed with a little herbed oil, and cooked for about 2 minutes, turning once. Large corn on the cob need their husks removed and need to be boiled for about 15 minutes. Drain, brush with herbed oil and wrap in foil. Place on the barbecue rack for about 15 minutes.

POTATOES

Small potatoes are the best size for barbecueing. Wash and dry before pricking each one with a fork. Brush with herbed oil and wrap in foil. Cook on the barbecue for about 1½ hours, turning occasionally. Remove the foil towards the end of the cooking time to allow the potatoes to crisp up a little.

ONIONS

Small onions are ideal but you need to boil them for about 10 minutes first. I prefer to leave their skins on, but it's a matter of taste. Be careful not to overcook the onions because they will disintegrate if they are too soft. Once threaded on skewers, onions will take about 10 minutes to cook on the barbecue.

Spiced Potato Salad

(6)

PREPARATION TIME: 10 minutes
COOKING TIME: 30 minutes

INGREDIENTS:
1½ lb/700 g potatoes, washed
6 tbsp low-calorie mayonnaise
1½ tsp curry paste
4 tbsp low-fat natural yogurt
1 tsp tomato purée

METHOD
1   Cook the potatoes in boiling water until just tender. Drain
    well and chop them. Leave to cool a little.
2   Mix together the remaining ingredients and pour over the
    potatoes while still warm.
3   Cool and serve.

Emerald Salad

(6)

PREPARATION TIME: 20 minutes

INGREDIENTS:
1 medium radicchio lettuce
1 small endive lettuce
½ medium Chinese leaf cabbage
½ medium webb lettuce
4 oz/125 g mangetout, topped
6 celery sticks, sliced
1 bunch watercress
4 oz/125 g green grapes, seeded

METHOD

1   Carefully wash all the ingredients and dry well.
2   Tear the leaves off the various lettuces if they are too large and place in a salad bowl with the remaining ingredients. Mix well.
3   This is particularly tasty served with a yogurt and herb dressing. Simply mix together some chopped herbs, such as parsley, rosemary and dill, with about 4 tablespoons of low-fat natural yogurt, black pepper and 2 teaspoons of garlic wine vinegar.

Fruity Salad

(8)

PREPARATION TIME: 10 minutes

INGREDIENTS:
1 red dessert apple, washed, cored and sliced
1 orange, peeled and sliced
1 pear, washed, cored and sliced
8 oz/225 g white cabbage, washed and shredded
1 tbsp fresh chives, chopped
6 spring onions, washed and chopped
1 tbsp pumpkin seeds

METHOD
Mix all the ingredients together well.

Herby Tomato Sauce

(¾ pt/400 ml)

PREPARATION TIME: 10 minutes
COOKING TIME: 7 minutes

INGREDIENTS:
2 tbsp olive oil
6 spring onions, finely chopped
3 garlic cloves, crushed
½ pt/275 ml red wine
2 tbsp garlic wine vinegar
2 tbsp tomato purée
1 tsp brown sugar
black pepper, freshly ground
1 tbsp basil, freshly chopped

METHOD

1 Heat the oil, add the spring onions and fry gently for 1 minute.
2 Add the garlic, red wine, wine vinegar, tomato purée, sugar, pepper and basil.
3 Bring to the boil and simmer for 4 minutes.
4 Cool, cover and chill in the refrigerator.

Sweet and Sour Sauce

(1½ pt/850 ml)

PREPARATION TIME: 10 minutes
COOKING TIME: 17 minutes

INGREDIENTS:
4 tbsp olive oil
1 onion, peeled and finely chopped
4 garlic cloves, crushed
6 spring onions, finely chopped
1 green pepper, seeded and finely chopped
1 orange pepper, seeded and finely chopped
2 carrots, thinly sliced
1 in/25 mm piece root ginger, grated
1 tbsp orange and lemon zest
1 ripe banana, chopped
6 tbsp garlic wine vinegar
½ pt/275 ml water
2 tbsp cornflour
1 tbsp tamari
black pepper and low-sodium salt

METHOD

1   Heat the oil in a frying pan and add the onion, garlic, spring onions, peppers, carrots and ginger. Fry for about 2 minutes before adding the zest and banana. Cook for a further 30 seconds.
2   Place the remaining ingredients in a bowl and mix together until smooth.
3   Add to the vegetables and bring to the boil, stirring continuously.
4   Simmer for about 15 minutes.
5   Serve hot.

Chilli Sauce

(¾ pt/400 ml)

PREPARATION TIME: 10 minutes
COOKING TIME: 7 minutes

INGREDIENTS:
2 tbsp olive oil
1 onion, peeled and finely chopped
¼ pt/150 ml tomato ketchup, low-sugar variety
2 tbsp Worcestershire sauce
1½ tsp chilli powder
¼ pt/150 ml garlic wine vinegar
1 tbsp clear honey
2 tsp wholegrain mustard
freshly ground pepper and low-sodium salt

METHOD
1 Heat the oil in a saucepan and gently fry the onion for 2 minutes.
2 Add the ketchup, Worcestershire sauce, chilli powder, wine vinegar and honey and bring to the boil. Stir in the mustard.
3 Simmer gently for 5 minutes before seasoning to taste.
4 Serve hot.

Barbecued Apples
(6)

PREPARATION TIME: 10 minutes
COOKING TIME: 30 minutes

INGREDIENTS:
6 large cooking apples, cored
2 tbsp broken walnuts
1 tbsp honey
1 tsp ground mixed spice
1 tbsp raisins

METHOD
1   Prick the apples with a fork.
2   Mix together the remaining ingredients.
3   Place each apple on a piece of lightly oiled foil about 10 in/25 cm square.
4   Press the honey mixture into the cavity of each apple and wrap the foil around them securely.
5   Cook over a hot barbecue for about 25 minutes, turning occasionally.

Hot Bananas
(8)

PREPARATION TIME: 1 minute

INGREDIENTS:
8 bananas

METHOD
Place the bananas, still in their skins, among the hot charcoal of the barbecue for about 5 minutes. Serve hot. If you like cinnamon, you could sprinkle a little on the bananas when peeled.

Fruit Kebabs
(8)

PREPARATION TIME: 10 minutes

INGREDIENTS:
2 oranges, peeled
1 red dessert apple, cored
1 green dessert apple, cored
2 bananas, peeled
16 mango chunks, 1 in/25 mm
2 oz/50 g low-fat cooking spread
1 tbsp honey
2 tsp ground cinnamon

METHOD
1   Cut each orange into 4 slices and cut each slice in half.
2   Cut the apples into 4 wedges.
3   Cut each banana into 4 pieces.
4   Thread 2 orange slices, 2 banana pieces, 1 apple wedge and 2 mango chunks on to each of 8 skewers.
5   Melt the low-fat cooking spread and stir in the honey and cinnamon.
6   Cook the fruit kebabs on a moderately hot barbecue for 5 minutes, turning and basting with the honey mixture frequently.
7   Serve hot.

PACK A PICNIC

I love picnics whatever the time of year and whatever the weather
– it must be the child in me, I think! Picnics are an adventure, an
informal fun-packed day out for all the family. And just look at
the scenery that is opened up to you: a quiet rugged beach with
sheer cliffs as the backdrop; a babbling brook bridged with step-
ping stones; a river with deep grassy banks; a windswept moor or
a wooded glade – the choice is yours to make.

Picnicking has always been an everyday part of my life both as a
child and an adult. A few years ago I asked four friends over to our
house for a long weekend with the Sunday earmarked for a picnic.
Sunday morning duly arrived and I was up very early enthusiastically packing all the food and paraphernalia. By the time the
others emerged for breakfast I was ready to go. Unfortunately,
the rest of the team were not. One look out of the window
convinced them that it was not a picnic type of day. The March
morning was cool, breezy and damp and dark clouds were gathering. Undeterred, I bullied them and packed large umbrellas,
windbreaks, waterproofs, anoraks and warm jumpers – just in
case! We had a great day. The moor I had chosen for our outing
was isolated but the strong winds weren't too bad once we had the
windbreaks securely in place. Yes, we shivered a little and huddled
up frequently to keep warm, and things did keep on blowing
away. But it all added to the fun. I wouldn't have missed that day
for the world – it was pure magic.

And what about that romantic picnic where your main aim is to
impress? A very good friend went to town on this particular picnic
with chilled wine, the lot. Unfortunately, it rained and so the
picnic was eaten in the back of the car. Busily tucking into the
food she remembered that she had something to get from the car
boot. Carefully, she placed the opened bottle of wine and two full
glasses on the back ledge of the car. The boot was opened, the
ledge jerked up, the bottle of wine and glasses fell off and spilt
down the back of her boyfriend. Quite impressive, don't you
think? Surprisingly they are still together!

But, that's the beauty of a picnic – you always come to expect
the unexpected.

BACK TO BASICS

A picnic can be anything you want it to be – romantic and intimate, planned or impromptu, formal or informal – but its very nature ensures that it is always an exciting adventure. The all-important point to remember about picnic food is that it must travel well. Ensure that the food you prepare is robust enough for the journey; fancy little vol-au-vents made from flaky pastry may seem a good idea but you could end up with a bag full of crumbs! Strong, rigid containers with tight-fitting lids are a must. Pack the food tightly, filling any gaps with crumpled paper or foil to avoid damaging collisions. Another safeguard is to pack the containers in a hamper, coolbox or even a cardboard box. I love the old-style elegant wicker hampers but coolboxes are more practical, especially on hot summer days. An effective way to cool wine is to tie a piece of string around it and dangle it in a nearby stream. You must make sure that it is secured to the bank, though! Essentials on a picnic are wet wipes, napkins, cutlery, plates, tablecloth, cushions to sit on and a container for your rubbish.

PACK A PICNIC

Menu

GAZPACHO

PITTA POCKETS
GREEN FINGERS
STUFFED TOMATOES
TUNA MOULD
MACKEREL AND ORANGE PÂTÉ
THE DOORSTOP SANDWICH
YOGURT POTATOES
LENTIL SALAD

APPLE TARTS
STRAWBERRY ROSE

Gazpacho

(8)

PREPARATION TIME: 20 minutes
COOKING TIME: 3 minutes
CHILLING TIME: 4 hours

INGREDIENTS:
2 onions, peeled and chopped
6 garlic cloves, peeled and crushed
1 red pepper, seeded and chopped
1 green pepper, seeded and chopped
1 yellow pepper, seeded and chopped
6 tomatoes, chopped
2 pt/1.2 l tomato juice
2 tbsp olive oil
freshly ground black pepper
low-sodium salt

METHOD
1 Put the onion, garlic, peppers, tomatoes, tomato juice, olive oil and seasoning into a blender. Blend until smooth.
2 Chill for about 4 hours or overnight.

Pitta Pockets

(6)

PREPARATION TIME: 15 minutes

INGREDIENTS:
6 spring onions, washed and chopped
3 tomatoes, washed and chopped
1 bunch watercress, washed and trimmed
2 oz/50 g black grapes, washed and seeded
4 oz/125 g Gouda cheese, chopped into small cubes
1 tbsp basil, freshly chopped
freshly ground black pepper
6 wholemeal pitta bread

METHOD
1   Mix together all the ingredients except for the pitta bread.
2   Cut each of the pitta breads in half and make each half into a 'pocket'.
3   Divide the salad mixture between the pitta pockets.

Green Fingers

(8)

PREPARATION TIME: 5 minutes

INGREDIENTS:
8 finger-like pieces of melon
8 slices gravadlax

METHOD
Wrap each of the melon fingers completely with the gravadlax.

Stuffed Tomatoes

(8)

PREPARATION TIME: 10 minutes

INGREDIENTS:
8 firm tomatoes, washed
3 oz/75 g white crab meat
2 oz/50 g low-fat cottage cheese
freshly ground black pepper
1 lemon, zest of

METHOD
1   Cut a slice off the top of each tomato and remove the seeds and pulp.
2   Mix together the remaining ingredients.
3   Divide the mixture equally between the tomatoes, then replace the tops.

Tuna Mould

(4)

PREPARATION TIME: 25 minutes
CHILLING TIME: 4 hours

INGREDIENTS:
6 oz/175 g tuna in brine, drained
2 tbsp dill, freshly chopped
1 tbsp chives, freshly chopped
4 spring onions, washed and chopped
1 carrot, washed and grated
freshly ground black pepper
½ pt/275 ml liquid aspic jelly

METHOD

1 Mix the tuna with the dill, chives, spring onion, carrot and pepper.
2 Mix the liquid aspic jelly with the tuna and pour into a 1 pt/550 ml mould.
3 Chill until set.

Mackerel and Orange Pâté

(6)

PREPARATION TIME: 20 minutes
COOKING TIME: 10 minutes
CHILLING TIME: 2 hours

INGREDIENTS:

4 oz/125 g polyunsaturated margarine, unhydrogenated
4 tbsp orange juice, sugar-free
1 lb/450 g mackerel fillets, boned and flaked
3 tbsp orange zest
¼ pt/150 ml fromage frais
freshly ground black pepper
low-sodium salt

METHOD

1 Melt the margarine and put in a blender with the orange juice and mackerel. Blend to a smooth purée.
2 Stir in the orange zest and fromage frais. Season to taste.
3 Spoon the mixture into a serving dish, cover and chill for at least 2 hours.
4 Serve with crusty bread.

The Doorstop Sandwich

(F 12)

PREPARATION TIME: 30 minutes plus 30 minutes proving time
COOKING TIME: 20 minutes
TEMPERATURE: 230°C/450°F/Gas 8

INGREDIENTS:

¼ pt/150 ml boiling water
½ pt/275 ml cold water
1 oz/25 g fresh yeast
25 mg vitamin C tablet, crushed
1½ lb/700 g wholemeal flour
2 tsp salt
2 tsp brown sugar
½ oz/15 g polyunsaturated margarine, unhydrogenated
2 tbsp poppy seeds

FILLING:

1 small tin of tuna in brine, drained and mashed
1 lemon, zest of
1 tsp low-calorie mayonnaise
4 tomatoes, washed and sliced

METHOD

1   Prepare the yeast liquid by mixing together the boiling water and the cold water then blending in the yeast. Add the vitamin C and stir until the powder has dissolved.

2   Put the flour, salt and sugar into a large bowl and rub in the fat. Add the poppy seeds.

3   Add the yeast liquid to the dry ingredients and mix to a firm dough. Knead until smooth.

4   Shape the dough into a ball and place in a lightly oiled polythene bag for 5 minutes. Remove the dough and divide into 12 portions. Cut each of the portions into 3 pieces and shape into fairly flat 3 in /7.5 cm discs.

5   Mix together the tuna, lemon zest and mayonnaise and place some of the mixture on one of the dough discs, cover with another dough disc and then a layer of the tomato, followed

by the final dough disc. Make sure that the edges of the 'round' are sealed together well. Repeat with the other discs. Put the rolls on a lightly greased baking sheet and leave to prove for about 30 minutes until doubled in size. Bake for about 20 minutes.

ALTERNATIVE FILLINGS:
Chicken with mushrooms and nutmeg
Low-fat cheese with spinach and garlic
Smoked fish with peppers
Garlic and herb low-fat soft cheese with spring onions
Prawns with low-calorie mayonnaise and endive

The variations are endless!

Yogurt Potatoes
(4)

PREPARATION TIME: 10 minutes
COOKING TIME: 20 minutes
CHILLING TIME: 1 hour

INGREDIENTS:
2 lb/900g small new potatoes
¼ pt/150 ml low-fat natural yogurt
1 lemon, zest and juice of
1 tbsp basil, freshly chopped
1 tbsp parsley, freshly chopped
freshly ground black pepper

METHOD
1   Wash the potatoes, and boil for about 20 minutes. Drain and leave to cool slightly.
2   Mix together the remaining ingredients and stir into the potatoes. Chill for about 1 hour.

Lentil Salad

(4)

PREPARATION TIME: 10 minutes
COOKING TIME: 30 minutes

INGREDIENTS:
8 oz/225 g red lentils, washed
1 onion, peeled and chopped
2 tbsp chives, freshly chopped
2 garlic cloves, crushed
1 tbsp garlic white wine vinegar
2 tbsp fromage frais
1 tbsp tomato purée
freshly ground black pepper

METHOD
1 Cook the lentils for about 30 minutes in boiling water and drain well.
2 Mix together the remaining ingredients and stir in the lentils. Leave to cool.

Apple Tarts

(F 6)

PREPARATION TIME: 20 minutes
COOKING TIME: 40 minutes
TEMPERATURE: 180°C/350°F/Gas 4

INGREDIENTS:
2 lb/900g red apples, washed, cored and thinly sliced
2 bananas, very ripe, mashed
1 tsp ground cinnamon
2 oz/50 g walnuts, broken
1 qty low-fat pastry (see p. 101)

METHOD

1 Mix together the apples, bananas, cinnamon and walnuts.
2 Setting aside a quarter of the dough, divide the remaining pastry into 6 portions and line 6 4 in/10 cm dishes which are about 1¾ in/4 cm deep.
3 Spoon the apple mixture into the tart dishes and use the remaining pastry to make the tops.
4 Prick the top of each tart with a fork and bake until golden brown.

Strawberry Rose

(6)

PREPARATION TIME: 10 minutes
CHILLING TIME: 2 hours

INGREDIENTS:
1 lb/450 g fresh strawberries, washed and hulled
1 tbsp rosewater

METHOD

1 Place 4 oz/125 g of the strawberries in a liquidizer with the rosewater and blend until smooth.
2 Mix the remaining strawberries with the sauce and chill for 2 hours, stirring occasionally.

THE GARDEN PARTY

The very mention of a garden party brings to mind a very grand occasion. For some obscure reason I always think of exquisitely dressed guests with posh hats being the order of the day, a game of polo taking place in the background, croquet on the lawn and champagne on ice by the gallon complete with strawberries! And of course the famous annual garden parties hosted by the royal family reinforce this image.

Such garden parties are not within my range of experience – as yet. But I'm working on it! Garden parties do tend to be quite formal occasions but this doesn't have to be the case at all. It's up to you to call the shots. A cautionary word is needed here, I think. Your idea of an informal garden party may be a good one but please remember to tell your guests in advance to save embarrassment on all sides. There is nothing worse than showing up to a 'do' in all your finery only to find that you are totally over the top.

BACK TO BASICS

A buffet-style arrangement is ideal for such occasions as it enables people to nibble, mingle and chat which, for me, is the essence of any garden party whether formal or informal. China crockery, linen napkins with 'proper' cutlery and glasses are essential – even if you have to beg, steal or borrow to acquire them. Please don't follow the path of a Lancashire lady who told me this true story.

Apparently, while living in Kenya she organized a garden party but didn't have enough china, cutlery and glassware. The house servant didn't see this as a problem. He nipped to the grand house next door and borrowed all their very best gear – including solid silver candlesticks. Everyone was enjoying the garden party when there was an unwelcome interruption. It was the local police. There had been a burglary next door . . . Yes, you've guessed it – the house servant hadn't told anyone what he was doing. And worst of all, these next-door neighbours weren't even invited to the garden party! Truth really is stranger than fiction, isn't it?

Some kind of informal seating arrangement is useful although you certainly don't need to provide seats for everyone. Some people will prefer to stand and others just to sit down for a while maybe while they eat. It is better to have a few tables rather than one large one for the food. And, to avoid confusion, place different courses on different tables and clearly mark them. I once made the mistake of eating a gooseberry fruit mousse with a savoury pancake because the dishes were mixed up and nobody knew what was what. The hostess was not too pleased with me nor with the countless others who made the same mistake.

It looks attractive to have crisp linen tablecloths with plenty of flowers decorating the buffet tables. The plates, napkins and cutlery should be ready for the guests to help themselves to. Another good idea is to have the drinks table well away from the food. You have probably noticed that people tend to gather around the drinks for a chat and nobody really wants to fight their way through to get to the buffet – after all, it's not a rugby scrum! Once again, as with any outdoor event, keep your eye on the weather and have an indoor venue ready just in case you have to make a mad dash!

THE GARDEN PARTY

Menu

CHILLED FENNEL SOUP
SUMMER SOUP

GARLIC AND CHEESE BREAD
CHEESE DIP
CREAMY MUSHROOMS

SALMON AND PRAWN MOUSSE
TUNA AND PRAWN FLAN
SPICED CHICKEN PIE
CHICKEN WITH MANGO
TURKISH TURKEY
CHEESE AND FENNEL TERRINE
RICE SALAD
CUCUMBER AND CHEESE RING
RATATOUILLE
SPINACH SALAD
GREEN LENTIL SALAD

FRUIT CHEESECAKE
CAROB MOUSSES
TIPSY FRUIT SALAD

COFFEE OR TEA

Chilled Fennel Soup
(F 15)

PREPARATION TIME: 15 minutes
COOKING TIME: 25 minutes
CHILLING TIME: 3 hours

INGREDIENTS:
4 fl oz/125 ml olive oil
4 lb/1.8 kg fennel bulbs, washed and chopped
3 large onions, peeled and finely chopped
4 pt/2.2 l vegetable stock
2 oranges, zest of
low-sodium salt
freshly ground black pepper
¾ pt/400 ml silken tofu, liquidized
1 tbsp ground black pepper
low-fat natural yogurt

METHOD
1 Heat the oil in a large saucepan and add the fennel and onions. Fry for 4 minutes, stirring frequently.
2 Add the stock, orange zest and seasoning. Bring to the boil, cover and simmer for about 15 minutes.
3 Place the soup in a liquidizer and blend until smooth. Stir in the tofu and black pepper and chill. Garnish with a swirl of yogurt.

Summer Soup

(122)

PREPARATION TIME: 20 minutes
COOKING TIME: 30 minutes
CHILLING TIME: 2 hours

INGREDIENTS:
2 bunches watercress, washed
4 tbsp olive oil
2 onions, peeled and chopped
4 pt/2.2 l skimmed milk
4 lb/1.8 kg peas, shelled or frozen
low-sodium salt
black pepper
½ pt/275 ml silken tofu, liquidized

METHOD
1 Chop the watercress roughly, reserving 12 sprigs for garnish.
2 Heat the olive oil in a saucepan and add the onion. Cook for 2 minutes. Add the watercress, cover and cook for 10 minutes, stirring frequently.
3 Remove from the heat and stir in the milk, peas and seasoning. Bring to the boil, stirring frequently.
4 Cover and simmer for about 20 minutes. Cool slightly.
5 Place in a blender and liquidize until smooth. Stir in the tofu. Chill well and serve garnished with watercress sprigs.

Garlic and Cheese Bread
(8)

PREPARATION TIME: 10 minutes
COOKING TIME: 10 minutes
TEMPERATURE: 190°C/375°F/Gas 5

INGREDIENTS:
1 large wholemeal French stick
2 oz/125 g polyunsaturated margarine, unhydrogenated
4 oz/125 g low-fat soft cheese
6 garlic cloves, peeled and crushed
black pepper
1 tbsp parsley, chopped

METHOD
1 Split the French stick in half lengthways and spread the cut surfaces on both sides with margarine.
2 Mix together the cheese, garlic, black pepper and parsley. Spread one side of the French stick with this mixture and sandwich together with the other half. Wrap in foil tightly.
3 Bake and serve either hot or cold cut into slices.

Cheese Dip

(12)

PREPARATION TIME: 5 minutes
CHILLING TIME: 2 hours

INGREDIENTS:
½ pt/275 ml fromage frais
3 garlic cloves, crushed
12 oz/350 g low-fat cottage cheese
4 oz/125 g Edam cheese, grated
2 lemons, zest and juice of
2 tbsp fresh chives, chopped
low-sodium salt
black pepper

METHOD
1 Combine all the ingredients very well.
2 Serve in small dishes with cocktail biscuits, oatbiscuits, crispbreads, vegetables or fruit.

Creamy Mushrooms

(12)

PREPARATION TIME: 15 minutes
COOKING TIME: 10 minutes
CHILLING TIME: 1 hour

INGREDIENTS:
5 tbsp olive oil
3 lb/1.5 kg button mushrooms, wiped
2 oz/50 g low-fat cooking spread
8 garlic cloves, crushed
4 tbsp plain wholemeal flour
2 fl oz/50 ml dry white wine
low-sodium salt
black pepper
soy sauce
4 fl oz/125 ml fromage frais, beaten
4 tbsp fresh chives, chopped
2 tbsp fresh dill, chopped

METHOD

1   Heat the oil in a large saucepan, add the mushrooms and cook, covered, for about 5 minutes. Stir frequently.
2   Drain, reserving the juices.
3   Melt the cooking spread in a pan, add the garlic and cook for a second or two. Add the flour. Stir in the reserved juices, wine, seasoning and soy sauce. Heat until the sauce boils and thickens. Simmer for 1 minute.
4   Add the mushrooms and fromage frais. Stir in the herbs.
5   Serve in small dishes.

Salmon and Prawn Mousse

(6)

PREPARATION TIME: 25 minutes
COOKING TIME: 25 minutes
CHILLING TIME: 3 hours
TEMPERATURE: 160°C/325°F/Gas 3

INGREDIENTS:
12 oz/350 g fresh salmon
1 oz/25 g low-fat cooking spread
1 oz/25 g polyunsaturated margarine, unhydrogenated
1 oz/25 g plain wholemeal flour
½ pt/275 ml skimmed milk
3 tbsp dry white wine
¼ pt/150 ml low-calorie mayonnaise
¼ pt/150 ml fromage frais
3 oz/175 g prawns, chopped
½ oz/15 g powdered gelatine
¼ pt/150 ml stock
1 egg white, whisked until stiff

METHOD

1 Place the salmon on a piece of foil greased with the cooking spread and wrap loosely. Cook for about 20 minutes. Allow to cool in the foil. Remove the skin and bones before flaking the fish. Reserve the juices.

2 Melt the margarine in a pan and stir in the flour. Cook for 1 minute, stirring continuously. Gradually add the milk, fish juices and wine and bring to the boil. Simmer for 2 minutes and allow to cool.

3 Beat in the salmon, mayonnaise, fromage frais and prawns. Dissolve the gelatine in the stock over a pan of hot water and add to the mixture.

4 Carefully fold in the egg white. Spoon the mixture into a mould or individual ramekins. Chill until set.

Tuna and Prawn Flan

(6)

PREPARATION TIME: 20 minutes
COOKING TIME: 45 minutes
TEMPERATURE: 190°C/375°F/Gas 5

INGREDIENTS:
1 qty low-fat pastry (see p. 101)
7 oz/200 g tuna in brine, drained
4 oz/125 g prawns
2 eggs, beaten
5 oz/150 g low-fat natural yogurt
low-sodium salt
black pepper
2 tbsp fresh dill, chopped
2 tsp anchovy essence
2 oz/50 g Gouda cheese, grated

METHOD

1   Roll out the pastry and line an 8 in/20.5 cm flan dish. Bake blind for about 10 minutes at 200°C/400°F/Gas 6.
2   Flake the tuna into a bowl and add the prawns, eggs, yogurt, seasoning, dill and anchovy essence.
3   Spoon the mixture into the flan case, sprinkle with the cheese and cook for about 30 minutes at 190°C/375°F/Gas 5 until set. Serve hot or cold.

Spiced Chicken Pie

(F 8)

PREPARATION TIME: 30 minutes
COOKING TIME: 2 hours
TEMPERATURE: 200°C/400°F/Gas 6

INGREDIENTS:
2 tbsp olive oil
1 onion, peeled and chopped
2 garlic cloves, crushed
1 tsp ground coriander
½ tsp ground allspice
2 lb/900g chicken, skinned and diced
¾ pt/425 ml chicken stock
3 bay leaves
1 tbsp fresh tarragon, chopped
black pepper
1 qty low-fat pastry (see p. 101)
2 oz/50 g dried apricots, washed and chopped
1 tbsp fresh oregano, chopped
beaten egg to glaze

METHOD

1   Heat the oil in a saucepan. Add the onion and garlic and fry for 3 minutes. Stir occasionally. Add the spices and chicken and cook for 5 minutes on a high heat, stirring continuously.

2   Pour on the stock and add the bay leaves, tarragon and pepper. Bring to the boil and simmer for 40 minutes.

3   Remove the chicken with a slotted spoon and set aside. Discard the bay leaves. Simmer the stock for about 20 minutes uncovered.

4   Divide the pastry dough into 2 portions, one slightly larger than the other. Roll out the larger one and use it to line a greased 10 in/25 cm pie plate. Prick the bottom with a fork.

5   Mix the chicken with the apricots and oregano and spread it over the bottom of the pastry case. Dampen the pastry rim.

6   Roll out the remaining dough and place on top. Seal the edges

and brush the top with beaten egg. Cut a hole in the centre and bake for about 40 minutes until golden brown.

7   Allow the pie to cool and then pour the stock through the hole in the lid. Serve the pie cold.

Chicken with Mango

(12)

PREPARATION TIME: 30 minutes

INGREDIENTS:
3 lb/1.5 kg chicken meat, skinned and cooked
2 ripe mangoes
2 green peppers, washed, seeded and chopped
1 orange pepper, washed, seeded and chopped
14 oz/400 g water chestnuts, tinned, drained and sliced
12 spring onions, washed and chopped
8 oz/225 g baby sweetcorn, washed and sliced
¾ pt/400 ml low-calorie mayonnaise
black pepper

METHOD
1   Cut the chicken into bite-sized cubes, and place in a large bowl.
2   Peel the mangoes and cut the flesh into thin slices.
3   Mix together the mango, peppers, water chestnuts, spring onions and sweetcorn.
4   Add the mayonnaise and season. Combine with the chicken and stir well before serving.

Turkish Turkey

(6)

PREPARATION TIME: 30 minutes

INGREDIENTS:
4 oz/125 g walnuts
4 oz/125 g toasted sunflower seeds
4 slices wholemeal bread, toasted
4 tbsp chicken stock
1 tsp paprika pepper
3 tbsp olive oil
4 garlic cloves, peeled and crushed
1 lemon, juice and zest of
low-sodium salt
3 tbsp yogurt
3 lb/1.5 kg turkey, cooked
12 black olives

METHOD
1 Put the walnuts and sunflower seeds in a liquidizer, blend for a couple of seconds only and remove. Break the bread into pieces and put into the liquidizer with the stock, paprika, oil, garlic, lemon juice, salt and yogurt. Blend until smooth.
2 Stir in the walnuts and lemon zest.
3 Chop the turkey into bite-sized pieces and combine with the walnut mixture. Garnish with the olives and serve.

Cheese and Fennel Terrine

(6)

PREPARATION TIME: 50 minutes
COOKING TIME: 1¾ hours
CHILLING TIME: 3 hours
TEMPERATURE: 180°C/350°F/Gas 4

INGREDIENTS:
1 lb/450 g fennel bulbs, washed and chopped
3 oz/75 g low-fat Roule cheese
1 lb/450 g Ricotta cheese
2 eggs
freshly ground black pepper
low-sodium salt
1 tsp fresh fennel herb, chopped
4 oz/125 g mangetout, trimmed and steamed for 2 minutes

METHOD
1 Grease and line the base of a 2 lb/900 g loaf tin.
2 Boil the fennel for 10 minutes in 3 pt/1.7 l of boiling water. Remove the fennel and retain the liquid. Make sure the fennel is dry by patting it well with kitchen paper.
3 Purée the fennel in a liquidizer and add the Roule cheese, Ricotta cheese, eggs, seasoning and half the fennel herb. Blend until smooth.
4 Pour half the puréed mixture into the prepared loaf tin. Arrange the mangetout on top, retaining a few for garnish, and cover with the remaining mixture.
5 Cover with greased foil and place in a roasting tin with enough boiling water to come halfway up the sides of the loaf tin.
6 Cook for 1¾ hours or until firm. Leave to cool before turning out.
7 Serve garnished with orange wings and mangetout.

Rice Salad

(6)

PREPARATION TIME: 10 minutes

INGREDIENTS:
8 oz/225 g long grain brown rice, cooked
6 spring onions, washed and chopped
1 red pepper, washed, seeded and chopped
½ ogen melon (or any other variety if you can't get hold of this),
peeled, seeded and chopped
1 bunch watercress, washed and broken
1 orange, peeled and chopped
2 tbsp fresh basil, chopped
2 tbsp toasted sunflower seeds

METHOD
Combine all the ingredients well.

Cucumber and Cheese Ring

(6)

PREPARATION TIME: 20 minutes
CHILLING TIME: 3 hours

INGREDIENTS:
8 oz/225 g low-fat soft cheese
¼ pt/150 ml low-calorie mayonnaise
½ oz/15 g powdered gelatine
¼ pt/150 ml fromage frais
1 cucumber, peeled and chopped finely
low-sodium salt
black pepper

METHOD

1 Mix together the cheese and mayonnaise. Sprinkle the gelatine over ¼ pt/150 ml water in a small bowl over a pan of hot water. Stir until dissolved. Cool.

2 Stir the cooled gelatine into the fromage frais and mix with the cheese and mayonnaise. Stir in the cucumber and mix thoroughly. Season.

3 Spoon the mixture into a dampened 1½ pt/1 l ring mould. Chill until set. Turn out and fill the centre with watercress, parsley or prawns.

Ratatouille

(8)

PREPARATION TIME: 30 minutes
COOKING TIME: 25 minutes
CHILLING TIME: 2 hours

INGREDIENTS:
2 aubergines, cut into slices
salt
4 tbsp olive oil
2 onions, peeled and sliced
4 garlic cloves, peeled and crushed
1 red pepper, seeded and sliced
1 yellow pepper, seeded and sliced
12 oz/350 g courgettes, sliced
8 oz/225 g tomatoes, chopped
8 oz/225 g mushrooms, wiped and sliced
2 oz/50 g tomato purée
½ pt/275 ml vegetable stock
black pepper
low-sodium salt
2 tbsp fresh chives, chopped

METHOD

1 Put the aubergine into a colander and sprinkle well with salt. Leave to drain for 30 minutes. Rinse and pat dry.

2   Heat the oil in a large saucepan. Add the onions and garlic and fry for 2 minutes, stirring occasionally. Add the aubergine and fry for 2 minutes before adding the peppers and courgettes. Cook for 2 minutes. Add the tomatoes and mushrooms and cook for a further 2 minutes.

3   Mix together the tomato purée and stock. Pour over the vegetables and season to taste.

4   Bring to the boil, cover and simmer for 15 minutes. Stir in the chives and cool. Serve well chilled.

Spinach Salad

(6)

PREPARATION TIME: 30 minutes

INGREDIENTS:
8 oz/225 g spinach, washed
2 oranges, peeled and chopped
6 spring onions, washed and chopped
2 oz/50 g walnuts, broken
2 tbsp fresh parsley, chopped
1 cucumber, washed and chopped

DRESSING:
1 tbsp garlic wine vinegar
2 tbsp sesame seed oil
2 garlic cloves, crushed
2 tbsp low-fat natural yogurt
1 tsp curry powder

METHOD
1   Mix together the salad ingredients.
2   Beat the salad dressing ingredients together well and pour on the salad just before serving.

Green Lentil Salad
(6)

PREPARATION TIME: 20 minutes

INGREDIENTS:
8 oz/225 g red lentils, cooked and drained
4 oz/125 g dried apricots, washed and sliced
4 tbsp fresh mint, chopped
4 tbsp fresh chives, chopped
2 tomatoes, washed and chopped
12 spring onions, washed and chopped
4 garlic cloves, crushed
4 tbsp lemon juice
2 tbsp sesame seed oil
low-sodium salt
black pepper

METHOD
Combine all the ingredients together well and serve.

Fruit Cheesecake
(8)

PREPARATION TIME: 15 minutes
COOKING TIME: 45 minutes
CHILLING TIME: 3 hours
TEMPERATURE: 180°C/350°F/Gas 4

INGREDIENTS:
1 lb/450 g Ricotta cheese
8 oz/225 g low-fat soft cheese
3 eggs
2 lemons, zest of
2 oz/50 g sugar
5 tbsp Greek strained yogurt
8 oz/225 g strawberries, washed and made into fans (see p. 53)
4 lime wings (see p. 52)

BASE:
3 oz/75 g low-fat cooking spread
1 oz/25 g oatmeal
1 oz/25 g sunflower seeds, toasted
3 oz/75 g wholemeal flour
1 oz/25 g sugar
2 tsp ground cinnamon

METHOD

1 Melt the cooking spread in a saucepan and stir in the remaining base ingredients. Cook for 2 minutes, stirring frequently. Press on to the base of a 7 in/18 cm loose-bottomed cake tin. Bake for 5 minutes.

2 Beat the cheeses until smooth, add the eggs one at a time and mix well. Add the lemon zest and sugar.

3 Pour this mixture on to the base and cook for 20 minutes. Spoon over the yogurt and cook for a further 20 minutes.

4 Cool for 3 hours in the tin. Remove and garnish with the strawberries and lime wings.

Carob Mousses

(12)

PREPARATION TIME: 15 minutes
CHILLING TIME: 2 hours

INGREDIENTS:
9 oz/250 ml plain carob 'chocolate' bars
2 oz/50 g light muscovado sugar
3 tbsp brandy
15 fl oz/400 ml Greek strained yogurt
15 fl oz/400 ml fromage frais
1 tbsp low-fat natural yogurt

METHOD
1 Break the carob into a heatproof basin and add the sugar and brandy. Place the basin over a pan of simmering water to melt the carob. Stir occasionally. Cool for 1 minute.
2 Mix the Greek yogurt with the carob mixture and fold in the fromage frais. Spoon into 12 glasses and chill for 2 hours. Swirl each dessert with low-fat yogurt.

Tipsy Fruit Salad
(12)

PREPARATION TIME: 20 minutes
MARINATING TIME: 3 hours

INGREDIENTS:
4 oz/125 g dried apricots, chopped
4 fl oz/125 ml *crème de cassis*
2 oranges, zest and juice of
2 oranges, peeled and chopped
2 red eating apples, cored and chopped
4 oz/125 g strawberries, washed, hulled and sliced
2 kiwi fruit, peeled and sliced
½ melon, peeled and chopped
4 nectarines, wiped and sliced

METHOD
1 Place the apricots in a bowl with the *crème de cassis* and leave to soak for 3 hours.
2 Put the remaining fruit in a serving bowl and stir gently to mix. Add the apricot mixture. Serve with Greek strained yogurt.

INDEX

afternoon tea 97–109
almonds: Ginger, Almond and Orange Shortbread 106: Pashka 72; Potato and Almond Croquettes 70
Amaretto: Kokuma 38
Animal Sandwiches 88
aperitifs 29
apple, dried: Granola Crunch 80
apple juice: Applejack 40
Applejack 40
apples: Apple Balls 53; Apple Tarts 186; Barbecued Apples 174; canapé toppings 123, 124; Fruit Kebabs 175; Fruity Salad 170; Mince Pies 147; Tipsy Fruit Salad 209
apricots, dried: Dundee Cake 105; Festive Loaf 138; Granola Crunch 80; Green Lentil Salad 206; Tipsy Fruit Salad 209
asparagus: Asparagus and Cheese Soup 68; Asparagus Sauce 74; canapé topping 124; Savoury Tartlets 118
aubergine: Ratatouille 204; Vegetable Kebabs 167

bain-marie 26–7
banana: Apple Tarts 186; Bananarama 96; Barm Brack 107; Fruit Kebabs 175; Hot Bananas 174; Passion and Banana Surprise 77; Stuffed Banana Pancakes 154
Barbecued Apples 174
barbecues 155–75; lighting for 156; tablecloths for 14; venues 156
Barm Brack 107
beef: wines to serve with 46
Betty's Tea Rooms 97
Birthday Cake 92
biscuits: Ginger, Almond and Orange Shortbread 106; Oatcakes 109; Orange and Currant Biscuits 95
Bloody Mary 36
Boxing Day dinner 149–54
brandy: Brandy Alexander 36; marinating peaches in 64
bread: Animal Sandwiches 88; Croûtons 53; Garlic and Cheese Bread 194; garnishes 53; Melba Toast 53; Not So Humble Sandwich 100; Pinwheel Sandwiches 89; Ship Sandwiches 88
Broccoli with Lemon 71
Bronx 37
Brussels Sprouts: Creamed 141
Bubbles 39
Bucks Fizz 34

cabbage: Fruity Salad 170
cakes: Barm Brack 107; Birthday Cake 92; Carob Cups 94; Christmas Cake 146; Dundee Cake 105; Fresh Cherry Ring 104; Fresh Strawberry Rounds 103; Rock Buns 108
canapés 120–4; bases 121; spreads 121–2; toppings 122–4
candles 22–3, 66
carob: Carob Cups 94; Carob Mousses 208
carrots: Carrot Roses 52; Carrots with Lemon 142; Carrots with Sultanas 71
celery: Celery Brushes 52; Emerald Salad 169
champagne: Bucks Fizz 34; Champagne Cocktail 37; Kir Royale 34; Kokuma 38; Peached 37
cheese: Asparagus and Cheese Soup 68; canapé spreads 121–2; canapé topping 124; chart of varieties 126–7; Cheese Balls 115; Cheese Dip 195; Cheese and Fennel Terrine 202; Cheese and Tomato Whirls 90; Cheese Twists 101; Cream Cheese Rounds 101; Cucumber and Cheese Ring 203; Doorstop Sandwich 184; Filo Rolls 117; Fruit and Cheese Sticks 116; Fruit Cheesecake 207; Garlic and Cheese Bread 194; Melon and Cheese Squares 125; Pashka 72; Pinwheel Sandwiches 89; Pitta Pockets 181; Potted Cheese 114; Ship Sandwiches 88; Stuffed Dates 116; Stuffed Prunes 117; Stuffed Tomatoes 182; Watercress Dip 114; wines to serve with 47
cheese and wine party 110–27
cherries: Fresh Cherry Ring 104
cherry brandy: Singapore Sling 35
chicken: Chicken Balls in Orange Sauce 151; Chicken Burgers 165; Chicken with Mango 200; Doorstop Sandwich 184; Marinated Chicken 164; Peppered Chicken 133; Prawn and Chicken Kebabs 161; Spiced Chicken Pie 199; Stuffed Boned Chicken 140; Stuffed Chicken Breasts 75; wines to serve with 46
chicken, smoked: canapé toppings 123
children: healthy eating 83–4
children's party 83–96; entertainment at 85; invitations 7; numbers to invite 84; safety at 84; serviettes for 15; tablecloths for 14
Chilli Sauce 173

Chinese food: wines to serve with 47
Chinese leaf cabbage: Emerald Salad 169
Christmas 127–54; decorations for 127; preparing food in advance for 129
Christmas Cake 146
Christmas Day dinner 137–47
Christmas Eve dinner 131–4
Christmas Pudding 144
Cinderella 39
citrus fruit: Citrus Butterflies 52; Citrus Twists 52; Citrus Wings 52; Citrus Zest 53
cocktails 33–40; alcoholic 34–8; non-alcoholic 39–40
coffee: making 43; types 42
Cointreau: White Lady 35
colour harmony: in menu 10
corn on the cob see sweetcorn
Country Rice 134
courgettes: Barbecued Courgettes 168; Courgette Cogs 51; Courgette Fans 50; Monkfish Kebabs 160; Ratatouille 204; Vegetable Kebabs 167
courses: number to serve 83
crab: canapé topping 122; Crab Ring 150; Savoury Tartlets 118; Stuffed Tomatoes 182
cranberries: Festive Loaf 138
crème de cacao: Brandy Alexander 36
crème de cassis: Kir 34; Kir Royale 34
Croûtons 53
cucumber: Cucumber and Cheese Ring 203; Cucumber Curls 51; Cucumber Fans 51; Not So Humble Sandwich 100; Spinach Salad 205
curaçao: Seawitch 38
currants see fruit, dried
cutlery: setting on table 25; using 12

dates: Christmas Cake 146; Christmas Pudding 144; Dundee Cake 105; Stuffed Dates 116
desserts: wines to serve with 47
Devilled Mushrooms 81
dips: Cheese Dip 195; Watercress Dip 114
drinks: after dinner 41; aperitifs 29; for children 95–6; cocktails 33–40; quantities required 111; wine 29–32; see also individual ingredients
drinks party 110–27
Dry Martini 38
duck: wines to serve with 46
Dundee Cake 105

Emerald Salad 169
engagement meal 67–72
endive: Doorstop Sandwich 184; Endive Delight 77

endive lettuce: Emerald Salad 169
etiquette 11–13

fancy dress parties 85
fennel: Cheese and Fennel Terrine 202; Chilled Fennel Soup 192; Mackerel with Orange and Fennel 162
Festive Loaf 138
filo pastry: Filo Rolls 117; Fish Wellington 68
finger bowls 24
fish: Doorstop Sandwich 184; Fish Ball Soup 132; Fish Cakes 163; Fish Wellington 68; wines to serve with 45
flans: Tuna and Prawn Flan 198
flowers: candles with 23; table decorations 23–4
food: colours 10; flavours 10–11; keeping hot 26–7; serving 26; textures 10
fromage frais: Carob Mousses 208; Cheese Dip 195; Mangetout with Smoked Salmon 120; Strawberry Cups 102
fruit: Fresh Fruit Jellies 93; Fresh Fruit Salad 82; Fruit and Cheese Sticks 116; Fruit Cheesecake 207; Fruit Kebabs 175; Fruity Salad 170; garnishes 52–3; Oriental Fruits with Tofu 135; Tipsy Fruit Salad 209; see also apples, bananas, etc.
fruit, dried: Barm Brack 107; Carrots with Sultanas 71; Christmas Cake 146; Christmas Pudding 144; Dundee Cake 105; Mince Pies 147; Orange and Currant Biscuits 95; Rock Buns 108

Galliano liqueur: Harvey Wallbanger 35
game: wines to serve with 46
garden party 188–209
Garlic and Cheese Bread 194
garnishes 49–54; bread 53; fruit 52–3; pastry 54; vegetable 49–52
Gazpacho 180
gin: Bronx 37; Dry Martini 38; John Collins 37; Pink Gin 34; Singapore Sling 35; Strega Crossward 38; White Lady 35
Ginger, Almond and Orange Shortbread 106
ginger ale: Ginger Refresher 40
glasses: table setting 25–6; types 40–1
goose: wines to serve with 46
Granola Crunch 80
grapefruit juice: Strega Crossward 38
grapes: Emerald Salad 169; Fruit and Cheese Sticks 116; Pitta Pockets 181
gravadlax: Green Fingers 181
Green Fingers 181
guests: matching 6–7; seating arrangements 27–8

haddock: Fish Wellington 68
Harvey Wallbanger 33, 35
herbal teas 43–4
Herby Tomato Sauce 171
hors d'oeuvres: wines to serve with 45

Indian food: wines to serve with 47
ingredients: healthy choices 55–9
invitations 7

Japanese food: wines to serve with 48
jelly: Fresh Fruit Jellies 93; Jelly Snow 94
John Collins 37

Kir 34
Kir Royale 34
kiwi fruit: Fresh Fruit Salad 82; Oriental
    Fruits with Tofu 135; Tipsy Fruit Salad
    209
Kokuma 33, 38

lamb: wines to serve with 47
lemon: Carrots with Lemon 142; Poppy
    Seed and Lemon Rolls 68
lemon juice: Cinderella 39; Pussyfoot 39
lentils: Green Lentil Salad 206; Lentil Salad
    186
lettuce: Emerald Salad 169
lime juice: Pussyfoot 39
liqueurs 41–2
Lotus Blossom 50
lychees: Oriental Fruits with Tofu 134

mackerel: Mackerel with Orange and
    Fennel 162; Mackerel and Orange Pâté
    183
mackerel, smoked: canapé topping 123;
    Fish Cakes 163
mandarin oranges: canapé topping 123
mangetout: Emerald Salad 169;
    Mangetout with Orange 152;
    Mangetout with Smoked Salmon 120
mango: canapé topping 124; Chicken with
    Mango 200; Fruit Kebabs 175; Mango
    Balls 53; Oriental Fruits with Tofu 135
Manhattan 36
Marinated Chicken 164
measurements: imperial/metric
    equivalents 61–2; North American
    equivalents 63
Melba Toast 53
melon: Green Fingers 181; Melon Balls 53;
    Melon and Cheese Squares 125; Rice
    Salad 203; Tipsy Fruit Salad 209
menu: balance in 10–11, 65; planning 5–6,
    9–11, 65–6
microwave cookers 27
milk: Bananarama 96; Strawberry Crush
    96

Mince Pies 147
mineral water: Applejack 40; Bubbles 39;
    Orange Flip 95
monkfish: Fish Ball Soup 132; Monkfish
    Kebabs 160; Monkfish and Prawn
    Ramekins 74
mousses: Carob Mousses 208; Salmon
    and Prawn Mousse 197
mushrooms: Creamy Mushrooms 196;
    Devilled Mushrooms 81; Festive Loaf
    138; Mushroom Burgers 90;
    Mushroom Catherine Wheels 49;
    Ratatouille 204

nectarines: Tipsy Fruit Salad 209
Not So Humble Sandwich 100

oatmeal: Oatcakes 109
oats: Granola Crunch 80
olives: canapé topping 124
onions: Barbecued Onions 168; Country
    Rice 133; Gazpacho 180; Ratatouille 204
onions, spring: Pitta Pockets 181; Rice
    Salad 203; Spring Onion Whisks 51
orange: Fresh Fruit Salad 82; Fruit Kebabs
    175; Fruity Salad 170; Ginger, Almond
    and Orange Shortbread 106; Mackerel
    with Orange and Fennel 162;
    Mangetout with Orange 152; Orange
    and Currant Biscuits 95; Spinach Salad
    205; Tipsy Fruit Salad 209
orange juice: Bucks Fizz 34; Chicken
    Balls in Orange Sauce 151; Cinderella
    39; Ginger Refresher 40; Harvey
    Wallbanger 35; Kokuma 38; Mackerel
    and Orange Pâté 183; Orange Fizz 40;
    Orange Flip 95; Pussyfoot 39;
    Screwdriver 37
oven temperatures 62–3

Pancakes: Stuffed Banana 154
parties 83–127; children's 83–96; drinks
    110–27; garden 188–209; tea 97–109
Pashka 72
Passion and Banana Surprise 78
pastry: garnishes 54; Low-fat Pastry 102;
    Pastry Flower 54; Pastry Shapes 54
Pâté: Mackerel and Orange 183
peach juice: Bubbles 39; Peached 37
Peached 37
peaches: marinating in brandy 64
pear: Fruity Salad 170
peas: Summer Soup 193
peas, split: Festive Loaf 138
Peppered Chicken 133
peppers: Baby Sweetcorn with Red
    Pepper 153; Barbecued Peppers 168;
    Doorstop Sandwich 184; Gazpacho

180; Ratatouille 204; Rice Salad 203;
Vegetable Kebabs 167
picnics 176–87
pies *see* tarts and pies
pineapple juice: Cinderella 39
Pink Gin 34
Pinwheel Sandwiches 89
Pitta Pockets 181
place settings 25–6
planning 5–7; making lists 8–9; menu 5–6,
9–11
Poppy Seed and Lemon Rolls 68
pork: wines to serve with 47
potatoes: Barbecued Potatoes 168;
Creamed Potatoes 152; Potato and
Almond Croquettes 70; Sautéed
Potatoes 143; Spiced Potato Salad 169;
Spiced Potatoes 76; Yogurt Potatoes 185
Potted Cheese 114
prawns: canapé topping 122; Doorstop
Sandwich 184; Fish Ball Soup 132; Monk-
fish Kebabs 160; Monkfish and Prawn
Ramekins 74; Prawn and Chicken
Kebabs 161; Salmon and Prawn Mousse
197; Savoury Boats 119; Stuffed Dates
116; Tuna and Prawn Flan 198
prunes: Granola Crunch 80; Stuffed
Prunes 117; Vegetable Kebabs 167
pumpkin seeds: Granola Crunch 80
Pussyfoot 39

rabbit: wines to serve with 46
radicchio lettuce: Emerald Salad 169
radishes: Radish Fans 51; Radish Roses 51
raisins *see* fruit, dried
Ratatouille 204
recipes: measurements 61
rice: Country Rice 134; Rice Salad 203
romantic dinner: menues 64–82; serviettes
for 15
rum: Rum Sauce 145; Strega Crossward
38

St Valentine's dinner 73–8
Salad Dressing 205
salads: Emerald Salad 169; Fruity Salad
170; Green Lentil Salad 206; Lentil Salad
186; Rice Salad 203; Spiced Potato Salad
169; Spinach Salad 205
Salmon and Prawn Mousse 197
salmon, smoked: canapé topping 123;
Mangetout with Smoked Salmon 120:
Not So Humble Sandwich 100
sandwiches: Animal Sandwiches 88;
Cream Cheese Rounds 101; Doorstop
Sandwich 184; fillings 100: freezing 98;
Not So Humble Sandwich 100;
Pinwheel Sandwiches 89; Ship
Sandwiches 88

sardines: canapé topping 123; Monkfish
Kebabs 160
sauces: Asparagus Sauce 74; Chilli Sauce
173; Herby Tomato Sauce 171; keeping
hot 26–7; Rum Sauce 145; Sweet and
Sour Sauce 172
Savoury Boats 119
Savoury Tartlets 118
Screwdriver 38
seating plans 27–8
Seawitch 39
serviettes: folding 15–22
serving food 26
shellfish: wines to serve with 46
Ship Sandwiches 88
shopping list 9
Singapore Sling 33, 35
smoking 24
soda water: Applejack 40; Orange Fizz 38;
Orange Flip 95
soup: Asparagus and Cheese Soup 68;
Chilled Fennel Soup 192; Fish Ball
Soup 132; Gazpacho 180; keeping hot
26–7; method of eating 12; Summer
Soup 193; wines to serve with 45
Spiced Chicken Pie 199
Spiced Potato Salad 169
Spiced Potatoes 76
spinach: Doorstop Sandwich 184; Filo
rolls 117; Spinach Salad 205
spirits: measures per bottle 111
Starfruit 53
strawberries: Fresh Fruit Salad 82; Fresh
Strawberry Rounds 103; Fruit and
Cheese Sticks 116; Fruit Cheesecake
207; Strawberry Cups 102; Strawberry
Fans 53; Strawberry Rose 187; Tipsy
Fruit Salad 209
Strawberry Crush 96
Strega: Seawitch 38; Strega Crossward
38
Stuffed Banana Pancakes 154
Stuffed Boned Chicken 140
Stuffed Cherry Tomatoes 125
Stuffed Chicken Breasts 75
Stuffed Dates 116
Stuffed Prunes 117
Stuffed Tomatoes 182
sultanas *see* fruit, dried
Summer Soup 193
sunflower seeds: canapé topping 124;
Granola Crunch 80
Sweet and Sour Sauce 172
sweetcorn: Baby Sweetcorn with Red
Pepper 153; Barbecued Sweetcorn 168;
Vegetable Kebabs 167

table: candles on 22–3; clearing 27; cloths
14–15, 98; finger bowls 24; flower

decorations 23–4; serviette folding
  15–22; setting 25–6
table manners 11–13
tablecloths 14–15
tarts and pies: Apple Tarts 186; Mince
  Pies 147; Savoury Boats 119; Savoury
  Tartlets 118; Spiced Chicken Pie 198;
  Strawberry Cups 102
tea: brewing 44; herbal 43–4; types 43–4
tea party 97–109
teapots: antique 97
temperatures: oven 62–3
Terrine: Cheese and Fennel 202
Thai food: wines to serve with 48
Tipsy Fruit Salad 209
tofu 55; Oriental Fruits with Tofu 134
tomato juice: Bloody Mary 36
tomatoes: Doorstop Sandwich 184;
  Gazpacho 180; Herby Tomato Sauce
  171; Pitta Pockets 181; Ratatouille 204;
  Stuffed Cherry Tomatoes 125; Stuffed
  Tomatoes 182; Tomato Cups 50;
  Tomato Flowers 50
Triple Sec: White Lady 35
tuna: Animal Sandwiches 88; Doorstop
  Sandwich 184; Stuffed Cherry
  Tomatoes 125; Tuna Mould 182;
  Tuna and Prawn Flan 198
turkey: canapé topping 123; Herbed
  Turkey Escalopes 166; Turkish Turkey
  201; wines to serve with 46
Turkish Turkey 201

veal: wines to serve with 47
vegans 8
vegetables: Barbecued Vegetables 168;
  garnishes 49–52; Vegetable Kebabs
  167
vegetarian food: wines to serve with 48
vegetarians 8
venison: wines to serve with 46
vermouth: Bronx 37; Dry Martini 38;
  Manhattan 36
vodka: Bloody Mary 36; Harvey
  Wallbanger 35; Screwdriver 37

walnuts: canapé topping 124: Stuffed
  Prunes 117
watercress: Emerald Salad 169: Pitta
  Pockets 181; Summer Soup 193;
  Watercress Dip 114
wedding anniversary breakfast 79–82
whisky: Manhattan 36
White Lady 35
wine 29–32; decanting 31; for drinks
  party 110–11; Kir 34; low-alcohol 32;
  measures per bottle 111; organic 32;
  pouring 31–2; serving sequence 31;
  serving temperatures 30–1; sparkling
  34, 37, 38; storing 30; what to serve
  45–8

yogurt: Bananarama 96: Carob Mousses
  208; Strawberry Crush 96; Yogurt
  Potatoes 185